# THE DISCOVERY OF TAHITI

# AN ACCOUNT OF
# THE DISCOVERY
# OF TAHITI

From the Journal of
GEORGE ROBERTSON
Master of H.M.S. Dolphin

Edited, with an Introduction by
OLIVER WARNER

With Wood Engravings by
ROBERT GIBBINGS

FOLIO PRESS : J. M. DENT
London 1973

Distributed for the Folio Press,
202 Great Suffolk Street, London, S.E.1 by
J. M. DENT & SONS LTD
Aldine House, Albemarle Street, London W.1

Folio Society first edition of 1955, printed
by letterpress, reprinted by photo-litho
in 1973

ISBN 0 460 04141 X

PRINTED IN GREAT BRITAIN
by The Pitman Press, Bath
Set in Poliphilus type
Bound by J. M. Dent & Sons Ltd, Letchworth

# INTRODUCTION

'THIS day', wrote the captain with a pardonable flourish, 'the Right Honourable the Lords of the Admiralty were pleased to Appoint me to the Command of his Majesty's ship *Dolphin*, lying in Dock at Deptford, where I went and hoisted a Pendant on Board, and began to enter Seamen.'

The day was 19 June 1766, early in the reign of George III. The *Dolphin* was a frigate, built to mount 24 guns, and copper-sheathed below the water-line, to keep her clear from barnacles. The captain's name was Samuel Wallis. He was a Cornish-man, a trifle under forty years old. Exactly a year after opening his Journal, he, and the hundred and twenty odd seamen whose names then filled the *Dolphin*'s muster-book, were to enjoy one of the most delectable adventures in history. They were to be the first Europeans ever to visit Tahiti. To say that they were received with open arms is exact truth, though their good fortune was preceded by at least one period of danger.

The *Dolphin* carried a young ship's company. The oldest man aboard was a quarter-master, Samuel Lawrence, who was forty-four. Officers apart, only seventeen men were over thirty. There was one Scot to every three Englishmen, and an Irish-man or a Welshman to every three Scots. There were two Americans, one West Indian, and a seaman from Madras. It was a representative muster and it was typical, like Captain Wallis, of the Hanoverian navy.

The first lieutenant's name was William Clarke. His own Journal is not very informative. Indeed the clearest, though not the most flattering, picture which posterity has of him is as 'Mr. Knowall' or 'Old Growl'. This is the guise in which he figures in the Journal of George Robertson, the frigate's sailing-master, which forms the substance of the present narrative.

The second lieutenant, Tobias Furneaux, was one of the several in the *Dolphin*'s company who followed the high tradi-tion of explorers by venturing more than once into uncharted

5

seas. He commanded the *Adventure*, a few years later, in Captain Cook's second circumnavigation, and he had a notable career as a fighting officer.

The *Dolphin* was blessed with a capable surgeon in the person of John Hutchinson: there were two Harrisons, William, the Gunner, who was a favourite with the first lieutenant, and John, the Purser, who was skilled in mathematics, and who was a friend of Robertson. The boatswain's name was Boxall. There were three master's mates and twelve midshipmen, some of whom kept Journals of the voyage. The most outstanding of these petty officers was John Gore. When the captain and the first lieutenant went sick it was he who, together with Furneaux and Robertson, was responsible for working the ship. Gore had already made one circumnavigation. He had been with Commodore Byron, the poet's grandfather, who had sailed the *Dolphin* across the Pacific in 1765. Scarcely was he home from his voyage with Wallis when he joined Cook in the *Endeavour*. With Cook he returned—no doubt with pleasure—to Tahiti. He then went to Iceland in command of a vessel chartered by Sir Joseph Banks. Finally, he served in Cook's last expedition and brought the ships home after the leader's death. In his later years he was regarded as the most experienced and practical officer in the entire navy.

Other interesting personalities were Robert Molyneux, a Lancastrian, and Richard Pickersgill, from Yorkshire. Molyneux later served as master of the *Endeavour*, but died during Cook's voyage. Pickersgill succeeded him, and sailed a second time with Cook, in the *Resolution*. Then—after having a spot of trouble with the Admiralty—he went into the privateering line, and was drowned in the Thames one evening as he was about to embark for a cruise.

At the time of the *Dolphin*'s commission under Wallis it was still believed that a large continent in the south Pacific remained to be discovered. Wallis's nominal orders were for the Leeward Islands, but these were a blind. 'Notwithstanding our Order of this date', wrote My Lords Commissioners of the Admiralty on

16 August 1766, 'you are hereby required and directed to proceed agreeable to the enclosed'.

The 'enclosed' were Secret Orders. They expressed 'reason to believe that Lands or Islands of great extent, hitherto unvisited by any European Power, may be found in the Southern Hemisphere between Cape Horn and New Zealand, in Latitudes convenient for Navigation, and in Climates adapted to the produce of Commodities useful in Commerce . . .' Although Byron had added little to geographical knowledge through his voyage, the *Dolphin* had proved her capabilities, and it was hoped that Wallis might have better luck.

Wallis had something in his favour. His service record was good, and he was particularly zealous for his seamen's health, on which much depended. Molyneux recorded that the organization of the ship was excellent, and that the men were 'as good a ship's company as ever sailed in H.M. service'. Nevertheless, four factors told against the larger purposes of the voyage. The captain had none of the zeal for pure exploration which the circumstances called for: by the time the *Dolphin* had tossed her way through the Straits of Magellan—the passage took no less than four months, which is a fact for the modern traveller to ponder—her people were in no fit state for immediate further exploits: Wallis himself was ill almost continuously from the time he entered the Pacific: lastly—as Cook was later to confirm, with infinite patience—there was in fact no great new continent to find.

Robertson and others in the frigate were deceived into thinking they had indeed sighted the shores of the fabled land. They were believed, and were ordered to keep silence as to its position: but all that had in fact been done was to discover Tahiti and to reveal, in that felicitous spot, an ideal place from which Sir Joseph Banks, and the astronomers with Cook, could later view the Transit of Venus across the sun.

If the main idea of the voyage was not realized, there were compensations. The first had nothing to do with the *Dolphin*. It was the astonishing circumnavigation made by Captain Philip Carteret of the *Swallow*, perhaps the pluckiest in history.

Carteret, another veteran of Byron's voyage, had accompanied Wallis from England, his sloop leaky and short-handed. He had battled his way to the western entrance of the Straits of Magellan. There the *Dolphin* and the *Swallow* parted company, and Wallis probably gave his consort up for lost. But courage made up for lack of equipment, and Carteret did at last bring the little *Swallow* home—in March 1769—after being overtaken in the South Atlantic by Bougainville. After an exchange of courtesies he was left by the French explorer, the second European leader to reach Tahiti, 'as if he had been at anchor'. The 'poor dull *Swallow*', as Robertson called her, was a slow sailer indeed, and her bottom was a mass of clinging growth.

The second compensation was the natural and ethnological excitement of Tahiti; the third was the small comedy of George Robertson, through which a present-day reader may recapture some of the original thrill of the island visit.

Robertson, who was probably a year or two younger than his commanding officer, was a first-rate navigator. His account of the passage through the Straits of Magellan, which appears in the fuller text of his Journal, is one of taxing emergencies and trials, cleverly surmounted. And at Tahiti it was he who got the *Dolphin* to safe anchorage, after she had grounded close upon her arrival; he who found, in Matavai Bay, the natural haven so often denied to hungry and thirsty mariners in the South Seas. Robertson reveals himself in his Journal as the perennial type of competent, respect-worthy, rank-conscious warrant officer—the back-bone of the naval calling, then and later.

Robertson apart, much of the interest of his story resides in nails and armourers. For the *Dolphin*'s people, when once they had beaten off the only planned attempt by the Tahitians to capture their ship, found all plain sailing. They traded and they loved. The price of love was paid in nails. When these ran short, the armourer and his mate were sent ashore with their forge to manufacture what they could. It was not before time.

'Found out', recorded Captain Wallis severely, on 20 July 1767, when his ship had been at Tahiti for a month, 'that Francis Pinkney had drawn the Cleats that the Main Sheet

8

was belayed to, and stolen the Spikes and thrown the Cleats overboard'. The sequel almost continued the comedy. 'Turned the people up,' said Wallis, 'shewed them what a Wanton Crime he had been guilty of, that many more must have been concerned in the like Theft, that they had as much Fresh Meat every day as they could Eat, and that the Price thereof was risen above Thrice its Value since we came here, occasioned by the Theft of these Large Nails. Then ordered them to prepare Nettles [1] and him to run the Gauntlet three times round the Deck, which he did, but was so tenderly treated that I told the People that they rather encouraged Thieves than prevented them ... Put a stop to any Person except the Guard from going Ashore again.' [2]

That was that: and in fact the *Dolphin* sailed a week later, the seamen no doubt torn between their wish to return home, the hope of fun arising from once more being allowed ashore, if the captain relaxed his orders, and—in Robertson's case at any rate—a hope, quickly to be dashed, that Wallis would permit himself an opportunity of penetrating the unknown land which they thought to be not far away to the southward.

In fact, Wallis continued to be ill. He sailed westerly, and, after a visit to the Ladrones and a necessary call at Batavia, made for the Cape of Good Hope and was back in England by the summer of 1768. He was in time to turn over charts, information and volunteers for the advantage of James Cook. His voyage was the prelude to a greater. Moreover, it provided a moral. For when he reached Tahiti in 1769, in the *Endeavour*, Cook made out five 'Rules to be observed ... for better establishing a regular and uniform trade for provisions etc with the Inhabitants ...' The fifth of these Rules ran: 'No sort of Iron or anything that is made of Iron, or any sort of cloth or other useful or necessary articles, are to be given in exchange for anything but provisions.'

[1] Nettles were made of twisted yarn, tightly bound to form a handle-less whip.

[2] Robertson's account of Pinkney's punishment, which differs slightly from the captain's, is entered under 21 July 1767.

9

In chronological sequence, the *Dolphin*'s progress was as follows. With the *Swallow* and the *Prince Frederick*, store-ship, she left Plymouth on 21 August 1766, 'victualled', says Robertson, 'with the best sorts of provisions that ever went to sea.' Captain Wallis, though senior officer, did not fly a broad pendant as commodore, as had Byron before him. He had orders to put in at Madeira for water, beef and onions, and the three ships were there between 7 and 12 September, the *Dolphin* departing with 'four Pipes and ten Puncheons of wine'. Molyneux adds: 'All human means have been taken to keep the ship's company healthy, namely: at our first coming out they were put to three watches, a thing very uncommon.' Current practice was apparently the exhausting watch-and-watch. 'So sensible were they of the favour', he says, 'that they all, to a man, exerted themselves to the utmost on every occasion.'

The next call, made on 24 September, was at St. Jago in the Cape Verde Islands, where they stayed four days, taking in water, purslane and bullocks. No sooner were they at sea again than the *Prince Frederick* reported leaks. Her men had to work the pumps continuously, and by the end of October they were exhausted, and beginning to go down with scurvy. Wallis sent his surgeon to do what he could for them.

By the middle of November the three vessels were off the estuary of the River Plate. They began to essay the Straits of Magellan on 17 December, having by then reached Cape Virgin, and they soon encountered the Patagonians, reported by Byron and earlier travellers as being of immense height. Carteret of the *Swallow* had two officers with him who, like himself, had been on Byron's venture, and their experience was now useful. Captain Wallis took a measuring rod ashore, to prove for himself this matter of height, and he found the men to be between six foot and six foot nine, which to the average British sailor of the day was tall indeed.

Wallis preferred the route through the Straits rather than the passage of Cape Horn. Due to the ever-prevalent danger of scurvy, his men needed to recruit their health with herbage only obtainable ashore. 'When we arrived', he wrote, 'all our people began to look pale and meagre; many had the scurvy to a great degree, and upon others there were manifest signs of its approach; yet in a fortnight there was not a scorbutic person in either of the ships. Their recovery was affected by their being on shore, eating plenty of vegetables, being obliged to wash their apparel, and keep their persons clean by bathing in the sea.'

On 17 January 1767 the *Prince Frederick*, having transferred stores to the *Dolphin* and *Swallow*, sailed east for the Falkland Islands, whence she made her way back to England. As for the two King's ships, their adventures in the rock-strewn, stormy Straits between 15 January and 11 April were a sequence of hardships and adverse weather, slowly surmounted.

On 11 April they reached the Pacific, at which point the *Swallow* was nearly wrecked, and was left behind, a shade unfeelingly as some in the *Dolphin* must have felt. Carteret had twice appealed to Wallis to let him exchange into the *Dolphin* as first lieutenant, so that Clarke could take his own dull vessel home, but Wallis would have none of it. When the ships lost touch in gale and, later, fog, Carteret recorded, with an absence of bitterness which does him credit: 'From this time I gave up all hope of seeing the *Dolphin* again till we should arrive in England, no plan of operation having been settled, nor any place of rendezvous appointed.' Wallis, so good in all which concerned the care of his men, never had a severer comment passed upon his abilities as senior officer.

In his traverse of the Pacific, upon whose waters he sailed with such relief, Wallis discovered various islands besides Tahiti. Loyalty seems to have been uppermost in his mind when he set about naming them. Tahiti itself became King George's Island. Murea, close by, was the Duke of York's Island; Mehetia, also in the Society group, was called Osnaburgh Island, after a German bishopric whose title was borne by one of the members of the Royal Family; and others who appeared on the captain's chart were Queen Charlotte, the Duke of Gloucester, the Duke of Cumberland, and Prince

William Henry. Nor was the Board of Admiralty forgotten. Lord Egmont, the First Lord, Admirals Saunders, Boscawen, Howe and Keppel—all illustrious in the Seven Years War— gave their names to islands or atolls which Wallis sighted but could not always visit. His final discovery—Uea in Samoa—he named after himself, and it is at this point that Robertson's narrative breaks off.

The *Dolphin* was at Tinian on 19 September. Her men were disappointed to find it less attractive than it had seemed to Anson when the expedition he commanded had put in there for refreshment a quarter of a century before. By that time the ship was handicapped through the fact that Furneaux, so invaluable at Tahiti and elsewhere, had joined the sick-list. Wallis stayed at Batavia for a week, from 30 November to 8 December; he was at Cape Town by 4 February 1768, and at anchor in the Downs by 20 May. Without question the frigate was a good sailer: equally without question Wallis, who received a gratuity of £500 and two years' leave, was glad he could hand over further tasks of exploration to more enthusiastic officers. His remaining service was in larger ships, and the last years of his life (1782–1795) were spent as Extra Commissioner of the Navy.

Robertson was deservedly promoted to commissioned rank for the notable skill he had shown on the voyage. Although he never became a post-captain, he was able, later, to serve his country actively in the War of the American Revolution. He seems to have seen the eighteenth century to within three months of its close, as a half-pay Lieutenant, and his memory must have been stored with a wealth of remarkable true stories.

III

Of Robertson's stories, that of Tahiti may well have been a general favourite, since from the time of the *Dolphin*'s visit the island was continually in the news. The French were quickly on the scene. Two ships under the orders of Bougainville lay off Hitiaa for just over a week in 1768. A year later the *Endeavour*'s craftsmen were busy repairing and sharpening iron tools left by Wallis among the islanders. Three years later still, in November 1772, a Spanish frigate, the *Aquila,* lay at the Dolphin anchorage for a month. The commander, Boenechea, had with him a Journal bought clandestinely from one of Wallis's seamen, who was then in the service of Spain. Boenechea was interested to observe that although French and Spanish colours meant nothing to the Tahitians, at the sight of a British ensign excitement was immediate and intense. Boenechea even had the curiosity to note in detail the marks on one of the *Dolphin's* hatchets: 'Crown brand: Quality A: Christopher Jones & Co'—thus, apparently, the inscription went.

Before the eighteenth century had run its course Cook was to visit Tahiti twice more, and the *Aquila* three times; moreover, the island was to become the scene of the demoralization of Bligh's crew, in H.M.S. *Bounty.* Bougainville thought of it as 'the new Cytherea': indeed, classicism was the garment in which many early descriptions were clothed. Philosophical theories were added, such as that of the Noble Savage which influenced so many so erroneously. Naturally there is no classicism in Robertson's and other nautical Journals, since they lacked the necessary background of scholarship; and reality, as the sailors could see, was otherwise. Indeed, an intelligent grasp of the paintings which were brought back to England by professional artists such as Hodges and Webber from Cook's two later voyages should have shown those with open minds that it was a strange and primitive way of life which Wallis had first broken in upon. Its roots would need to be sought by the scientist far beyond the confines of Europe. Even today, the matter is by no means settled.

The first land sighted by the *Dolphin's* look-outs after once beating clear of the Magellan Straits were islands of the Tuamotu archipelago. No landing was possible, and although on 18 June Maitea—in the Society Group—was in sight all day, and the barge and cutter were sent to prospect, once again it proved impossible either to water the ship or to obtain provisions.

Tahiti, seen on 19 June, had at first the appearance of part of the sought-for continent. As by that time the captain and the first lieutenant were suffering severely from the stomach troubles which laid them low so persistently, and as there were at least thirty men bad with scurvy, hopes of succour ran high. On 21 June the ship did in fact anchor in seventeen fathoms, and next day the men began to trade. But it was not until two days later, after the frigate had struck on what was later known as the Dolphin Bank and been brought off without much harm, that they were anchored securely at Matavai, known to them henceforward as Port Royal Bay.

Trials were not quite over. From the first, the Tahitians had been fascinated by any objects made of iron, which metal they did not possess. Great thieves, on 24 June they made their one big attempt to capture the ship, together with the limitless iron which they may well have thought to be aboard. Canoes surrounded the *Dolphin*. In each, young girls stood up, making enticing gestures, and when the men judged that the time was ripe, they closed, hurling stones at the British vessel. Little harm was done; and as Wallis had taken the precaution of bringing up some of the big guns from the hold, the invasion was soon scattered with artillery, which the *Dolphin*'s officers used with creditable reluctance. The assailants were driven off with loss. Henceforward there was no serious danger, for the Tahitians realized the power of the people they had now encountered.

Robertson's narrative gives a clear and delightful account of events covering the remainder of the time that his ship was at Port Royal Bay, including a close view of the local Queen, and relating some amatory adventures which art could scarcely improve. Robertson was not, so it appears, personally involved. This seems right for a man of his exemplary comportment— but his descriptions leave the reader in no doubt about how much the other Dolphins enjoyed themselves.

It is sometimes said that Wallis's discipline was lax. This was not so. In the Journal of Ben Butler, who may well have been responsible for administering punishments, under the direction of the officers and the master-at-arms, floggings are recorded on 25 June, and on 5, 19 and 20 July—these in addition to Pinkney's running of the gauntlet on 20 or 21 July. Another Journal records one further flogging, on 2 July. The offences were cheating the natives, disobedience and drunkenness, the worst offender being a corporal of marines, who was beaten twice.

The Dolphins were in truth well disciplined, well looked after, and full of the traditional gaiety of the sailor. They would have spread lively tales, on their return home, of the joys of island life; but few accounts could convey more graphically and individually the incidents of Tahiti than the Journal of the simple navigator whose impressions, with all their oddity, their imperfection and their vitality, lose nothing from the passage of the years.

Robertson made a few mistakes, naturally enough. It was not, for instance, the 'king of the Island' who led the attack on 24 June, but more likely priests; and Queen Purea, known later to Cook as Queen Oberea, did not lose her husband by the fire of the ship's guns, as Robertson seems to have thought. But by and large, not much missed or deceived him, and his narrative is worthy of an astonishing interlude in the hard lives aboard a frigate of the reign of George the Third.

It would have been an appropriate rounding-off to this account could it have been recorded that Captain Wallis, when he had the British colours hoisted at Tahiti on 26 June 1767 and drunk to the future of King George's Island in rum mixed—in moderation—with the excellent local water, added a permanent speck to the British Empire of the future. But it was not so.

After the sailor-explorers, of varying nationalities, came the missionaries. At first they were under the patronage of the Matavai chief Pomare, though that monarch was not himself a Christian. His son, Pomare II, was driven from the island in 1809 and the missionaries also left. The king returned six years later, a declared convert. He was baptized a few years later.

In 1816 two French Catholic priests arrived, but were

15

expelled. The French Government acted sternly. They demanded an apology, an indemnity, and a most-favoured-nation treaty, and in 1843 accepted the offer to make the island a French Protectorate, the British having more than once declined a similar opportunity. In 1880 Tahiti was declared a French colony, which it has since remained. Bougainville's countrymen, second in the line of discovery, proved more tenacious than those of Wallis the pioneer.

### EDITOR'S NOTE

*My thanks are due to the President and Council of the Hakluyt Society for their courtesy in allowing the reproduction of that part of the text of* The Discovery of Tahiti—*edited by the late Hugh Carrington, 1948—which concerns the island itself. The Journal of George Robertson of* H.M.S. Dolphin, *which forms the substance of the Hakluyt Society's publication, has been followed with few omissions, and those purely technical. Robertson's narrative has been supplemented here and there with details from the Journals of other members of the ship's company which are now—apart from that of Robert Molyneux, which is in the Egmont Papers in the British Museum—in the Public Record Office. The spelling and punctuation have been modernized for the convenience of the present-day reader.*

O. W.

# THE DISCOVERY OF TAHITI

*19 June* THE Wind at ENE a Moderate Gale and clear weather over-head, but hazy in the Horizon all round. At 2 P.M. we made sail and steered WSW ½ W. Our greatest hope at this time was the prospect of high Land, which we all supposed we saw the day before. This was the only Comfort we had for departing so soon from Osnaburg Island, and thanks be to the Almighty we was not disappointed in our hopes.

At 3 P.M. we saw the Land bearing W ½ S. It appeared to be a great high mountain covered with clouds on the top; at 6 A.M. the Extreme of this Land bore from W ½ S to W by N ½ N distance about 14 Leagues: at the same time we saw the tops of several mountains the Extremes bearing from South to SW upwards of twenty Leagues. This made us all rejoice and filled us with the greatest hopes Imaginable; we now looked upon our-selves as relieved from all our distresses, as we were almost Certain of finding all sorts of refreshments on this great Body of Land, Especially as there was so great plenty on Osnaburg Island, which was only a small detached spot in comparison with what we saw this evening at Sun Set. We now supposed we saw the long-wished-for Southern Continent, which has been often talked of, but never before seen by any Europeans.

19

In order to prevent our being embayed, the Captain ordered us to steer for the Northernmost land in sight: at sun-set Mr Furneaux and I was both at the mast-head and most of the young Gentlemen all Looking out for shoals but saw none. This made us venture to run until 10 P.M., which was near the distance that we could discover any shoal; we then Lay-to and Earnestly wished for a New Day.

At 2 A.M. the Weather being very clear we made sail and steered WSW ½ W until sun-rise, when we saw the Extremes of the Land bearing from WNW to NW by N about 5 Leagues. We then altered our course and steered right in for the Land. At this time the weather was very thick and hazy all round, so that we could see no more of the Land to the Southward. At 9 A.M. we was obliged to lay-to, the weather being so thick and foggy that we could not see the Land altho' within two Leagues of it. This thick weather made us all very uneasy for fear of falling in with some shoal, especially as we heard the sea Breaking and making a great noise, on some reefs of Rocks which lie off the E. end of this Land.

In a short time the fog cleared up, and we saw the Easternmost point of this Land bearing N. two Leagues, at same time saw breakers betwixt us and the shore—and upward of a hundred canoes betwixt us and the breakers all paddling off towards the ship. When they came within pistol shot they lay by for some time—and looked at our ship with great astonishment, holding a sort of Counsel of war amongst them: meantime we made all the friendly signs that we could think of, and showed them several trinkets in order to get some of them on board.

After their Counsel was over they paddled all round the ship and made signs of friendship to us, by holding up Branches of Plantain trees, and making a long speech of near fifteen minutes. When the speech was over he that made it threw the plantain branch in to the sea, then they came nearer the ship, and all of them appeared cheerful and talked a great deal but none of us could understand them, but to please them we all seemed merry and said something to them. Their language is not Guttural but they talked so very fast that we could not distinguish one word from another. The nearest resemblance that I know to it, is the Patagonians' Language.

By this time we had upwards of a hundred and fifty canoes round us, and a great many more still coming off from the shore. In the canoes there was about Eight hundred men. By this time I suppose they thought themselves safe, having so many of them about us, and we still making friendly signs and showing them trinkets. One fine brisk young man ventured on board the ship; he came up by the mizen-chains and Jumped out of the shrouds upon the top of the awning, where he saw none of us standing. We made signs for him to come down on the Quarter-deck and handed up some trinkets to him, but he Laughed and stared at us and did not receive anything from us, until several of the Indians along-side made Long talks and threw in several Branches of plantain Trees. After throwing in the Plantain Trees, which is an Emblem of Peace, he accepted of a few trinkets and shook hands with us: soon after several of them came on board but we gave nothing to any but he that came first.

They seemed all very peaceable for some time, and we made signs to them, to bring off Hogs, Fowls and fruit and showed them coarse cloth, Knives, Shears, Beads, Ribbons etc, and made them understand that we was willing to barter with them. The method we took to make them Understand what we wanted was this: some of the men Grunted and Cried like a Hog, then pointed to the shore—others crowed Like cocks, to make them understand that we wanted fowls. This the natives of the country understood and Grunted and Crowed the same as our people, and pointed to the shore and made signs that they would bring us off some.

We then made signs for them to go in their canoes and to bring us off what things we wanted. They observed what we meant, and some went into their canoes, but the rest began to pull and haul at the Iron stanchions and Iron ring-balls in order to carry them off, and seemed greatly surprised that they could not Break them. We showed them some nails, which

21

they appeared very fond of; in short they seemed very fond of everything which they saw made of Iron, and began to be unwilling to go out of the ship without some Iron-work.

At this time there was a great number of their canoes alongside, and they began to be a Little surly. This made us fire a nine-pound shot over their heads in order to frighten them in their Boats. This had the desired Effect and all of them Jumped overboard and swam to their canoes. All the canoes paddled about a hundred yards from the ship, and Lay there until all their people swum on board. One of the fellows was standing close by one of our young Gentlemen, Henry Ibbot, who wore a Gold Laced Hat. This Glaring Hat attracted the fellow's fancy, and he snatched it off and Jumped overboard with it in his hand. When he got about twenty yards from the ship, he held up the Hat and wore it round his Head. We called to him and pointed muskets at him, but he took no notice of the muskets, not knowing their use. When this fellow got to the canoe he belonged to, all of them began to paddle towards the ship. I suppose they would have tried for more prizes, but we prevented them by making sail and standing offshore. When they saw we sailed faster than they could paddle they all returned to the shore.

[Captain Wallis's Journal fills out a further detail of this first encountering of the Tahitians. 'As one of the Indians was standing near a gang-way,' he recorded, 'one of our goats butted him upon the haunches. Being surprised at the blow, he turned hastily about, and saw the goat raised upon his hind legs ready to repeat the blow.' He jumped overboard.

Possibly this was the doughty goat that, having survived a circumnavigation in the *Dolphin*, lived to grace Cook's *Endeavour*, and to end his days in the odour of sanctity as an in-pensioner of Greenwich Hospital, his collar bearing an inscription composed by Doctor Johnson.]

$\text{T}_{\text{H E}}$ Wind was at E by N & ENE, a Moderate Gale and Cloudy hazy weather. After a short Consultation we Bore away to the Westward, in hopes of getting some place to Anchor in, where the ship could lie in safety. While we was running down along-shore we kept a very strict look out at the mast-head for shoals, but saw none, but a Great Reef of Rocks which runs along-shore, at about two miles Distance from the shore. This Reef has several large Openings in it, where there appears to be plenty of Room, and water for any ship to go in at—and within the Reef there appears to be Deep Water, and plenty of room to Anchor a Great Number of ships if the Ground is Good.

At 3 P.M. we brought-to abreast of a large Bay where we supposed there was good anchoring. We hoisted out the Cutter, and Mr Gore was ordered to go in her manned and Armed and to sound this Bay. They set out immediately and soon got close to the Reef, where a number of Canoes came round them, which paddled after our Boat. When the Cutter got near the place where they were Ordered to sound, we observed a Great Number of Canoes surrounding her, which made us suppose they meant to Attack her. The Captain therefore Ordered her signal to be made, and fired a nine-pounder; this was immediately observed by Mr Gore and he directly put about and stood off towards the ship.

When the natives saw him stand in they gave him no trouble—but the Instant they Observed him standing towards the ship, they all Endeavoured to cut him off from the ship: but the cutter being a fine clean Boat sailed faster nor they could paddle, and none of them had sails. He got soon clear of the most of them, but a few which was full of men way-laid the cutter and threw some stones, which hurt some of the cutter's hands.

Mr Gore then seeing their intention, fired at the Man he saw throw the first stone and wounded him in the Right shoulder, which prevented him from throwing any more stones. All the rest of the canoe's crew Jumped overboard, which put all the other canoes in great Disorder, and our cutter got safe on board and we hoisted her in. Just as we was going to make sail, we observed a large canoe under sail standing off to the ship. We supposed this to be some chief's, or a message from some head Man, as we saw none of the rest with sails. We waited for her; she appeared to sail very fast and soon got along-side, but we saw no person of Distinction in her—but one of the men made a short talk, and threw on board a Branch of a plantain Tree which we understood as the Emblem of peace—therefore made a short talk, and threw him in another which we got before, and the Captain Gave him some toys which seemed to please him much. While this canoe lay along-side the fellow that stole the hat came and wore it, but we made sail and stood off before he could reach the ship. We supposed the fellow wanted to deliver it Back for something Else—but that's uncertain.

All the way that we ran along-shore we saw the whole coast full of Canoes, and the country had the most Beautiful appearance it's possible to Imagine. From the shore side, one two and three miles Back, there is a fine Level country that appears to be all laid out in plantations, and the regular-built Houses seem to be without number; all along the Coast, they appeared like long Farmer's Barns, and seemed to be all very neatly thatched, with Great Numbers of Cocoa-Nut Trees and several other trees that we could not know the name of all along the shore.

The Interior part of this country is very Mountainous, but there are beautiful valleys between the Mountains. From the foot of the Mountains half way up the Country appears to be all fine pasture land, except a few places which seemed to be ploughed or Dug up for planting or sowing some sort of seed. From that to the very tops of the Mountains is all full of tall Trees, but what sort they are I know not, but the whole was Green. This appears to be the most populous country I ever saw, the whole shore-side was lined with men, women and children all the way that we sailed along. We was not fully persuaded that this was a part of the southern continent, we therefore Determined to work to windward all night, for fear of being embayed between this north shore and the High Mountains which we saw last night to the southward of us.

24

The weather still kept thick and hazy to the Southward so that we saw nothing but the appearance of the high mountains through the clouds. At A.M. we tacked and stood to the N by E six Leagues, but saw nothing of the land; we therefore Tacked and Stood to the Southward, until day light, then tacked and stood to the Northward and weathered the East end of the Land.

At Noon we observed the Easternmost point of the land S by W four miles, and a small key or island about two mile to the Eastward of said point bearing S ½ W, and the Northernmost Land in sight bearing NW by W five leagues. The East end of the Land Appears to be as full of houses as the South Side, and the Inhabitants Appear as Numerous on the beach, but none of them attempted to come off to us—but we saw several Large sailing canoes coming in out of the sea from the NW. Where they had been or What they were about I know not; some of them bore away when they got in our Wake, but never came so near us that we could see what was in their canoes.

They appear to sail about one fourth faster nor our ship when we made all the sail we could conveniently carry. Between the East point of the Island and the Northernmost point which we saw at noon there is a Bay about four Leagues Deep. The Houses here seem to be larger and longer than any of the rest, and the Inhabitants are very numerous, and the country in the bottom of the Bay has the most beautiful appearance. It is not near so high as the east end of the land, and appears to be all pasture-land—except a few miles from the beach that's full of cocoa and other trees. This ought to be the Winter Season if any such there be—but there is not the least Appearance of it to be seen; all the Tall trees is Green to the very top of the Mountains.

[An entry under this date in the Journal of Mr. Douglas, the Carpenter, is of significance, in view of certain events which were to follow. 'An Indian', he says, 'Snatched a Cleat that had a nail in it and jumped overboard and swam off.']

**21 June** THE Wind was from ESE to East, a moderate Gale and fine pleasant weather. We keep running along the North side of this Land at about three miles distance from the shore. When we was abreast of the Northernmost side of the Bay which was last mentioned, we saw two small islands which sheltered a very fine Roadstead; if there is good Ground

in it the place looks well here. We saw several canoes running along Shore but none of them came off to the ship.

At 4 P.M. we was abreast of a fine pleasant valley where we saw great numbers of houses, and the appearance of several very good plantations, we likewise saw the appearance of a fine Large River here, and observed some of the canoes that was sailing along stop here. We supposed these sailing canoes was running express to alarm the coast. I generally kept at the mast here to Look out for Shoals, but saw none. We sounded frequently but found no ground, but I observed the water change colour about a mile within us, which made me suppose there was sounding. This I acquainted the Captain with, but he did not choose to hoist out a boat to try it then.

Soon after we got abreast of a low point of land where we found the coast branch away to the SW, and saw very high land to the westward about six leagues. Round this low point of land I saw the appearance of a fine bay with white water in it, a sure sign of good anchoring ground. This I informed the Captain of but it was then too late to go in to sound this bay; we therefore triple Reefed our top-sails and kept working to windward all night, in hopes of finding a good safe anchoring place in the morning.

At this time our Captain and first Lieut. was both bad, and about thirty seamen in the Doctor's list, some of which was so bad, that he Expected Death to seize them soon, if timely relief was not found, on this pleasant and delightful country.

We passed most of this night in various reflections according to the Different dispositions of the people. The Greatest part of the Ship's Company made sure of finding all sorts of refreshments, and looked upon all the Difficulties of procuring them to be nothing. Others supposed nothing could be had without blows, and made a great many idle suppositions, with respect to the savage Disposition of the natives: and some thought it impossible to Land here, the natives being so numerous, and thought it best to run to Tinian, it being a place where we was sure of procuring all sorts of Refreshments, without running the least risk of Losing either our lives, Ship or Boats; and to attempt to Land here, or anchor any way near the shore, where thousands of their canoes could surround us, it was supposed to be the Greatest risk of Losing the ship and all of us. But happily for the sick and Afflicted, it was resolved on to try landing here, before we bore away for Tinian, which we afterward found to be four thousand two hundred and forty six miles from this country—so that if we had been so silly, as to set out for Tinian, we should have arrived in as great Distress, as the late Lord Anson did if not worse,[1] besides the disagreeable reflection of seeing a fine beautiful country full of Inhabitants, that was never discovered by any European before this date, and not being able to give our King and Country a proper and Distinct Account of it, altho' sent for that purpose.

When Day Light Appeared the Barge and Cutter was hoisted out and both Boats Manned and Armed. Then the Captain Ordered me to go and sound the Coast for Anchoring Ground. This I complied with and set out immediately. I went in the Barge and Mr Gore in the Cutter. The instant we set out from the ship we saw great numbers of Canoes set out from the shore, and steering towards us. When I saw this, in order to prevent accidents, I ordered Mr Gore to keep sounding, and I lay close by him with the Barge to prevent the Natives from interrupting him from sounding.

When we got within about two and a half mile of the shore, we found thirty fathom Water, fine Black sandy Ground within two cable lengths of the shore. When we got in amongst the canoes they all waved us off and seemed Greatly enraged when we stood in for the shore. When we found no regular soundings and all fine Black sandy Ground, we made the signal to the ship, that we had found good Anchoring Ground. This they observed and stood in to seventeen fathom, where the ship Anchored in fine Black sandy Ground, and veered to a whole cable on the best Bower, the Extremes of the Land in sight bearing from ESE to NW by W, distance off shore about two miles.

When the ship anchored I returned on board and acquainted the Captain what sort of sounding we found betwixt the Ship and the Shore. By this time several of the canoes came alongside with cocoa-nuts and several other sort of fruits, a few fowls and some fine fat Young Pigs, and our people and them had begun to trade, but all the country people behaved very insolently; none of them would trust any of our men with any of their things until they got nails or toys from them; then several

[1] Anson was at Tinian for two months (26 August to 21 October) in 1742, on his famous voyage of circumnavigation (1740–1744).

of them would push off and keep all: and others carried their insolence so high that they struck several of our men. This our seamen was very unwilling to put up with, but the Captain having given strict orders, that no man should hurt or molest them, until we tried their tempers, this made our men put up with their ill behaviour for a short time.

Soon after I returned to the ship the Captain Ordered me to go and sound along-shore, and to look out for a proper watering place. By this time there was several thousand of the natives assembled on the shore-side, upward of a hundred Canoes along-side, and near twice that number betwixt us and the shore, several of them large double canoes with long prows, and Eight twelve and sixteen men in Each. All the Large Canoes carried sail, but the small ones all paddled. The very instant that we set out in the Barge and Cutter, all the large sailing canoes set out after us, and hooted and made a great noise, which with their insolent behaviour on board made me suspect they had some design on us. I therefore told Mr Gore in the cutter to keep on his guard—and I should keep close by him, as we sailed best in the Barge.

In a few minutes the sailing canoes came up with us, and kept so near us that we both found it impossible to sound. We therefore made all the sail we could and left off sounding, in order to look for a convenient Watering-place; but several of the large canoes still came up with us, and some of them Attempted to board our Boats, but we avoided them and kept clear for some time—still making all the friendly signs that we could think of, and frequently waving to them to keep off.

But they, supposing we was afraid of them, still behaved with. more insolence—indeed I must own we had some reason to be a little afraid, for by the time we got close to the shore there was above two hundred great and small canoes round us, and near fifteen hundred men in them. As to the numbers that was on the shore, of men, women and children, it was impossible to form any idea of them, the whole Coast was lined with them as far as we could see.

When we got close to the shore we saw the Entry of a fine

River, but no water for a Boat to go in to it, and the surf run so high all along shore, that no man could Land with his Arms dry. We ran a little way along shore in hopes of being able to sound, but they crowded so thick about us that we found it impossible. While we ran along shore, the natives waved to us to come ashore, but they being so numerous and those in the canoes so insolent I thought it more prudent to return on board as I found it impossible to do the duty that I was ordered.

The instant that we tacked and stood off all the people ashore set up a loud cry, and those in the canoes began to hoot at us—and several of them attempted to board us, and seemed greatly enraged at us when they found we would not land. When we got within a mile and half of the ship—one of the Large Canoes run aboard of the Cutter, and carried away her boomkin and tore the mizen—but they soon got clear of her by using the picks and Bayonets. At the same time another attempted to board us, but we soon got clear of him. A few minutes after, three of the largest Attempted to board us all at once. I then ordered the Marines to point the muskets at them, but they Laughed at us, and one struck his prow right into our Boat's stern, and four of the stoutest fellows immediately Jumped on the prow of the canoe, as if they meant to board us, with their paddles and clubs in their hands.

When I found them so very resolute, I ordered one of the marines to fire his musket right across their canoe, in hopes of frightening them, without doing them any more hurt; but this had not the desired Effect, it only startled them a little, and when they found none of them was hurt, they all gave a shout and run directly for our boat's stern again, and the other two came right for the middle of our Boat, fully resolved to board us, which, if they had, their prows would have certainly sunk our boat, and all of us must have inevitably perished.

At the same time they were attempting to board the cutter. I then found it was too late to treat them with tenderness, especially as the ship took no manner of notice of us, altho' they saw the whole transaction very plain. Had there been a nine-pound shot fired over their heads, perhaps it may have frightened them from hurting us. But that not being done, I thought myself under a necessity of using violent means, I therefore ordered the serjeant and one of the Marines, to wound the two most resolute like fellows, that was in the boat which first Boarded us. This order was Complied with, and the one was killed which the serjeant fired at, and the other was wounded in the thigh, and both fell over-board.

When the other fellows in the canoe saw this they all Jumped over-board, and the other two Canoes immediately steered off. When we pointed the muskets to them they held up their paddles before their faces and dropped astern clear of us—and when they saw we gave them no more trouble, the crew of the Canoe that first boarded us all Jumped into their canoe and hauled in the two men that was wounded. One appeared quite Dead; they tried to make him stand, and when they found he could not, they endeavoured to make him sit, but found he was quite dead. Then they Laid him down in the bottom of the canoe, and one of them supported the other, and the rest made sail and stood in for the land.

After this none of them Attempted to come near our Boats, and we soon got On board, I then told the Captain my Reason for not sounding, and likewise informed him that it was impossible to Land, any way near Pleasant Valley without Wetting the people's Arms. He then asked what was best to be done, and I proposed going to examine the bay which we saw the night before, as that was on the lee side of the low point, where there was a great probability of Landing with our arms dry, besides a very great chance of Anchoring in a fine smooth bay with the ship. The Captain seemed very agreeable to this proposal, but soon after rejected it, being otherways advised by another officer—who proposed Anchoring farther in and bringing the ship's Broadside to bear on the River Mouth, and to keep a constant firing into the Woods, until we got our water complete, then to set out for Tinian. If we had wanted nothing else but Water this method might have done, altho' not without a great deal of danger.

31

**22 June** THE Wind from E to SE by E, a moderate Gale and Cloudy with some Rain. This day several Canoes came off with Hogs, Pigs, Fowls and fruit of various kinds such as plantains, Bananas, Bread fruit and some other fruits whose names I know not. We purchased the whole for nails and other trifling things. The most of the natives traded very honestly— but a few of them was very great Rogues, and frequently attempted to defraud our men, by going off with the nail or toys without paying for them; but pointing a musket or even a spy-Glass at them, they would return the nails etc. or give Value.

They now understood the use of Musketry and made signs that we had killed two of their partners. The way they took to make us understand them was this; they called loudly bon-bon,[1] then smote their breasts and foreheads and laid backward with their eyes fixed and without motion. The Market price for this day was a twenty-penny nail for a Hog of about twenty pound; a tenpenny for a roasting pig; a sixpence for a Fowl or a bunch of fruit, or a string of Beads would purchase a fowl or some fruit, but all of them seemed most fond of nails.[2]

This day Mr Gore was ordered to take the Barge and Cutter Manned and Armed, and to sound the Coast along to find out a watering-place, and to land if possible. If the natives gave him any trouble he was ordered to come off immediately, and the ship was to fire some round shot amongst them. Our boats set out and found fine regular soundings from 17 to 5 fathom, all fine Black sandy Ground. When they got in-shore they found the surf running very high, and saw no place where any man could land, without endangering his life, as well as spoiling fire-arms, which was the only thing we had to depend on, if the natives proved troublesome.

[1] Possibly imitative of the bang of the guns.

[2] In the eighteenth century nails were sold at so many pence per hundred. Thus tenpenny nails cost tenpence a hundred. Compared with modern nails a fivepenny nail is $1\frac{1}{2}$ in.; a tenpenny nail, $2\frac{1}{4}$ in.; twenty-penny nail, 3 in.; thirty-penny nail, $3\frac{1}{2}$ in.; forty-penny nail, $4\frac{1}{2}$ in.

None of their canoes Attempted to come near our boats, but great numbers of men and women assembled on the Beach, and made signs for our men to land; but they very prudently deferred landing at this time, but made the natives understand that we wanted water, and showed them toys and nails to encourage them to bring some off. At last some of the natives ventured off through the surf, with large bumbards and cala-bashes [1] full of Water. They swim like fish, and dive much Quicker nor any can believe without seeing them. I this day tried several of them by throwing a nail in the sea, and they dived and catched it along-side the ship—several times. At noon Mr Gore returned with about twenty Gallons of very Good Water.

*23 June*  THE Wind was Easterly, a moderate Gale and cloudy with some Rain. Mr Gore was ordered to take gang Casks and Breakers [2] in the Boats, and to do all he could to get the natives to bring off water. For that purpose he got nails of all sorts and pieces of Iron hoops, to pay them with; at 4 P.M. the Boats returned with only four Breakers of Water. When they got in-shore the natives came off and took six Breakers ashore to fill; but could not be prevailed on to bring more than four off. Our men made all the friendly signs they could think of, to get them to return the Breakers, but all in Vain, they would not, but made signs for our men to Land and they would haul their Boats up in the Woods.

When our people could not prevail by fair means, they began to threaten them by pointing the Muskets at them, but that they made game of and Laughed very hearty, not knowing that the Muskets could hurt them at so great a distance. This made Mr Gore fire a Musquetoon along shore, that they might see the Balls take the water, at a greater distance than they were from

[1] *Bumbard:* a cask or large vessel for liquids. *Calabash:* the shell of gourd or palm.

[2] *Gang-casks and breakers:* small barrels used for bringing water on board boats: gang-casks, the larger, held 32 gallons.

the Boats. This he thought would make them sensible of the danger they were in, but this had not the desired Effect; they only started back a little at the report, but seemed to take no notice of the Balls.

They soon found none of them was hurt, and all returned back to the Water-side, and brought a good many fine young Girls down of different colours. Some was a light copper colour others a mulatto and some almost if not altogether White. This

new sight Attracted our men's fancy a good deal, and the natives observed it, and made the Young Girls play a great many droll wanton tricks, and the men made signs of friendship to entice our people ashore, but they very prudently deferred going ashore, until we turned better acquainted with the temper of this people.

When our Boats returned with only four Breakers, which is but forty Gallon at most, we found it impossible to water by the assistance of the Natives. Our water was now very short and not near a sufficiency to carry us to any known place, therefore

34

some said it was absolutely necessary to get water at any event, and others said it was now impossible, as the Natives must now be greatly enraged against us, especially as I had now killed two of them. To this reflection I gave a very concise Answer by telling these two men, that what I had done I was ready to do again if necessity required it; if my own Life or the lives of those committed to my care be in danger, I always think it a duty incumbent on me to Extricate both, out of all the difficulties that's in my power.

The Captain now being very bad and not able to keep the Deck, he consulted with his Officers what was best to be done. Our first Lieut. was likewise bad and not able to do duty upon Deck, but thought himself very Able to Advise. What Advice he gave the Captain at this time I know not, but I afterwards found it was Opposite to mine, at a time when it hurt me greatly. But I believe it turned out to be for the good of us all, as it made me do what I should not have done so willingly at Another time. This makes the old proverb Good, that evil designs is sometimes productive of Good. I should not have mentioned this had it not been to clear myself of some reflection which this knowing man made afterwards.

But to be short with this affair, the most of us thought it best to weigh, and run down to the Leeward of the low point, where we saw the appearance of Anchoring ground, and smooth water to land with our boats, that no man needed to be afraid of wetting his feet, much less his Arms. This was agreed on, and we Weighed: our plan was this; to run down under the lee of the point, and there to lie-to with the ship until we sounded the Bay with the Boats. If any great number of the Natives Assembled round us in the canoes, the ship was to keep so near them that she could throw a shot over them to frighten them and prevent them from hindering us sounding the Bay. If we found good Anchoring Ground the ship was to be carried in; if no Anchoring, we was to return back and Anchor within a short mile of the River Mouth, and there make the best shift we could under the cover of the ship's Guns.

When we got near the point we went ahead with the Boats.

I kept nearest the shore in the Barge, and Mr Gore kept about two Cable lengths without me in the Cutter; both kept Constantly sounding. When we got a little round the point we saw several thousands of the Natives assembled on the shore, and a great number of canoes in the Bay, which we intended to sound. This made the ship stand close in after us, to prevent the canoes from hindering us to sound the Bay. This surprised me greatly as the ship was not to come nearer us nor a mile until I made the signal for Anchoring.

By this time she was so near that I called to them to keep off, as I had only three fathom, but they being nearer the Cutter, who had plenty of Water, did not observe what I said. Soon after the ship struck, and stood fast on a reef of rocks, which put all on board in great confusion. The Instant she struck the ship came head to Wind and I thought she was in stays,[1] and kept sounding on for some time, until they called to me from the ship and desired me to come on board. By the time I got on board the ship was paid round off, with the wind on the Beam, and her head to the sea, which made me still think her in safety, but this was owing to her drawing Nineteen or twenty Inches more forward nor aft. It seems she swivelled round on a rock forward and her stern swinged in. When I got on board I found her strike several times very hard, and all the sails Aback or shaking in the Wind.

By this time the Captain had given orders to clear the Decks of all lumber, which was immediately done and the people was busy in getting in the stream cable and Anchor to heave the ship off. The Captain and first Lieut. was now on deck giving orders, I therefore applied to the Captain for orders to do that which was best for the safety of the ship, but before the Captain could give me a proper Answer, Mr Knowall interrupted him, and told me on the public Quarter-deck, that this misfortune was entirely owi⟨n⟩g to my wholesome Advice, and now I should know the danger of Contradicting him. When we shall be soon in the Enemy's power I should know better.

[1] Robertson thought the ship was in process of changing tack, going about and technically 'in stays'.

This speech made my heart ache—but the time was improper to Answer him as he deserved. I therefore told him we would find another time to dispute that point, but now was the time to study the safety of the ship. I therefore desired the seamen to fill all the sails, as the ship's head was to the sea; at the same time I asked the Captain if he Approved of what I did. He said he did, but Mr Knowall disapproved of this, and laid hold of the Weather fore-Brace to haul it in, but his strength was not Equal to his ill nature, and no man assisted him.

At this Instant the men at the Lead said the ship drew ahead; this gave great joy to all on board but to me in particular. In a few minutes we got Clear off, and run out about a Mile. We frequently sounded the pumps but found she made but very little water more than usual. While we was on the reef we fired a few Guns to prevent the Natives from Attempting to come near the ship, until we got clear off from the shore, we then lay-to and I went down to the Captain and earnestly solicited him, to let me make another trial of sounding the bay, which he readily agreed to, and sent up orders to man the Boats.

While I was getting orders from the Captain, Mr Knowall ordered Mr Gore to go in the Barge and sound off the Low point, and ordered the Cutter for some other use, and told me there was the Jolly-boat for me to go where I wanted to go, as she drew least water I would run the less risk of losing her. At first I resolved to acquaint the Captain but he then being so bad in his health and greatly the worse for being upon Deck, I thought it wrong to hurt him more—and desired Mr Knowall to order the Jolly-Boat to be manned, and I went down to my Cabin to write a few Lines as I was doubtful of returning back to the ship. In a few minutes I was sent for and told the Boat was ready. I immediately put on a pair of good pistols and took my Broad-sword in my hand without the scabbard. My friend Knowall met me and told me the Boat had been waiting me some time; I told him it was very well, I was now ready to go in her, small as she was. In this Boat I had only five of the smallest lads in the ship, which was her proper Crew, and no Arms for any of the five, and two marines with their muskets. With this stout crew I set out to sound what we afterwards called Port Royal Bay [Matavai Bay]—where there was about two hundred canoes.

The instant I set out the ship made sail and stood off about three or four miles from the shore before she tacked. In standing in some of the people said we was in soundings, and Mr Knowall ordered the Anchor to be let go; it immediately ran out about fifty or sixty fathom before the stoppers was put on; at same time the ship drove, and the Anchor hung up and down: all the sails was lying unfurled, and the man at the lead said he had no ground with forty fathom line. Then the Deep sea lead was taken, and no ground found with a hundred and twenty fathom line. Then Mr Knowall ordered the Anchor to be hove up.

At this time I was amongst the Canoes, and all of them staring at me, several of them came round me and some were so near that I had not room to throw the Lead. I then Expected they would run us down or board us every minute—but in hopes to frighten them I ordered the two Marines to point their muskets at them. This made them sheer off a little, but soon after one old cross-like fellow began to call out to his fellows and sheered close to us. I threatened him by pointing the Muskets at him but he held up his paddle and sheered off again so that I was able to sound, and found fine regular soundings within a Cable length of the shore.

This made me very happy and all that was in the Boat. The poor youngsters said there was no Danger to be feared from the Natives; I then gave them a dram of good old Rum each, but the instant we turned towards the Ship, which was now without Gun-shot of us, a Great Number of the canoes surrounded us and seemed resolved to attack us. I then expected the Barge would come down to our assistance, and ordered one of the Marines to fire amongst the thickest of the Canoes. This made the most of them sheer off, but one fellow that threw a stone at us but luckily hurt none of us. I immediately fired a pistol at this fellow, which I believe went through his paddle, which he

38

held up before his face, as I afterwards saw him show the paddle to several other canoes.

This made them all keep off, but the Barge never came near us which surprised me greatly, and I never yet learned the Reason why she did not come to assist me, both to sound this fine Bay and protect us from the Natives: but very fortunately for us the Captain observed us with his Glass out of the Cabin window, and ordered the ship to stand in, and fired several shot at the Barge—in order to make her come down to us: but they say they did not understand that signal—however it was of great use to me and the poor little Jolly-boat's crew. The Natives were again surrounding, which obliged me to order another musket to be fired amongst them, which with the great Guns so terrified them that they all dispersed.

Mean-time the Captain ordered the Cutter manned and Armed to my assistance. By the time she reached me I crossed the Bay twice and found it all good Ground. I therefore Ordered the Young Gentleman in the Cutter to take the Jolly-Boat, and row up to the Barge and order her to come down and lie on the end of the shoal which the ship struck on, in order to be a mark for me to steer in by.

At same time I rowed off to the ship in the Cutter, and acquainted Capt. Wallis what sort of a Bay I had found out. He desired to know the reason that I went down without the Barge, and I told him Mr Knowall knew that best, but if he pleased I would take Charge of the ship, and carry her in to the finest Bay I ever saw, where there appeared to be a small River, where we could have no manner of Difficulty in Completing our water. This pleased him a good deal but he was still doubtful about the shoal. I told him the Barge and Jolly-Boat was both now upon the outer end of the shoal, so that there was no kind of Danger in going in to the Bay. He then ordered me to take charge of the ship and carry her in. I then ordered them to steer right in, keeping the two Boats a little open on the Larbord Bow—and I stood at the fore-top-mast-head where I saw the shoal as plain as if I had been upon it. In a short time we Anchored in 17 fathom Water, fine white sandy ground.

[At this stage of the visit, with one great danger surmounted, and more anticipated, Captain Wallis records that he put the ship's company at four watches, 'one always under arms'.]

*24 June*  THE Wind was Easterly with fine Moderate clear weather. Run out three hundred fathom of Hawsers and warped the ship farther in to the Bay, where we moored with the Best Bower and stream anchor in fifteen fathom Water, fine White sandy Ground.

From Noon to sunset several canoes came off with Hogs, pigs and fruit, which we purchased for toys and nails. While we was trading with those that brought off refreshments of all sorts, several other canoes came off and viewed us, frequently paddling round the ship. At sunset we armed every man with a pistol and cutlass, and Loaded the great Guns, some with round shot, and others with Grape shot. The Gunner and the three mates had the charge of the four Watches. We likeways loaded all the small arms. This was a fine clear pleasant night, but we neither saw nor heard any of the Canoes pass nor repass all the night, but we saw a great number of Lights upon a great reef of Rock that lies off the SW point of this Bay. This alarmed us a little, not knowing what they might be about, but we afterwards found they were fishing with some sort of torch Light.

At sunrise about three hundred canoes came off and lay round the ship, as many as could conveniently lay alongside traded very fair and took nails and Toys for their Hogs, fowls and fruit. By Eight o'clock there was upwards of five hundred canoes round the ship, and at a Moderate Computation there was near four thousand men. The most of the trading canoes which lay round the ship, and dealt with our people, had a fair young Girl in Each Canoe, who played a great many droll wanton tricks, which drew all our people upon the Gunwales to see them. When they seemed to be most merry and friendly some of our people observed great numbers of stones in every canoe. This created a little suspicion in several of our people, but the most of us could not think they had any Bad Intention against us, Especially as the whole traded very fair and honest, and all the men seemed as hearty and merry as the Girls.

At this time the whole Bay was all lined round with men, women and children, to see the Onset which was now near at hand, but they still behaved friendly until a large double canoe came off from the shore, with several of the Principal Inhabitants in her. This canoe lay some time on the Larbord side but kept a good distance from all the rest, and was observed to hoist some signal by some of our men. The very instant that this signal was made all trade broke up, and in a few seconds of time all our Decks was full of Great and small stones, and several of our men cut and Bruised.

This was so sudden and unexpected by the most of us, that we was some time before we could find out the cause, therefore ordered the sentries to fire amongst them, in hopes that would frighten them, but this had not the desired Effect. They all gave another shout and poured in the stones like hail amongst us, which hurt a great many of our men. We then found lenity would not do, therefore applied to the Great Guns, and gave them a few round and Grape shot, which struck such terror amongst the poor unhappy crowd that it would require the pen of Milton to describe, therefore too much for mine.

When any of the round shot took their canoes it carried all before it, and the poor unhappy creatures that escaped immediately Jumped overboard and hung by the remaining part of the canoe, until some of their friends took them up or towed off the Broken canoe. When we found they all pulled off, we gave over firing for some time, and enquired how this affair began.

In the mean-time all the canoes began to Assemble together at about a mile distant from the ship, thinking themselves safe from all danger, not knowing how far our shot could reach. By this time we all found out how this affair happened, and several of the Young Gentlemen and Common seamen pointed out the Great canoe which gave the signal to the rest, to begin the Onset. We afterwards found out that the King of the Island

41

and several of the Grandees was in this canoe,[1] who now began to Rally his forces at about a mile distant without the ship, and several other large double canoes Rallied the Canoes at about a mile distant within us. We then thought it full time to disperse them, and make them sensible of the danger they were in, in order to deter them from making any more attempts upon the ship, and as the poor Unfortunate King was in the Boat which first Attacked us, we resolved to prevent him and his friends in the Boat, from Attempting any such thing again, therefore pointed two Great Guns at this Great Canoe, well loaded with round and Grape shot, which soon drove her in two and I believe few that was in her Escaped with life.

But what surprised me most was the resolution of five or six small Canoes, with only four and six men in Each, who Constantly lay close by their King, and great men, when all the rest fled as fast as they could paddle off. These few poor fellows behaved so brave, that they not only carried off the Lame and Dead Men, but they even towed off the two shattered ends of the canoe to the end of a reef.

We fired a few shot at the remaining part of the Great Canoe, after she was in tow, and one of the round shot struck on part of her, but even this did not make this handful of Brave men give over their good offices to their chiefs and leaders. When they Landed on the Reef we gave over firing, and the poor men carried up the Lame and Dead Men, and I suppose gave them a decent Burial. While this was doing the Great Canoes in-shore had assembled above three hundred canoes and began to paddle towards the ship. I believe these Generals knew nothing of the fate of their King, or they would not have made another Attempt, for two Guns made them give up, and paddle off with all the strength they had.

But this far I must allow they Judged Wisely in Dispersing as fast as they possibly could—for we let them come within about three or four hundred Yards of the ship, then fired a three-pounder Loaded with seventy Musket Balls amongst the thickest of them; this made them all sheer off, not without a

---

[1] The attack was in fact led by a priest.

considerable Loss, and to add the more to the terror they were in we fired two round shot amongst them when they were about a mile from the ship: this made them all paddle off with all their strength, and the whole of them Landed, and we gave over firing and got up the Eight Guns which we formerly stowed in the hold, and Mounted them in their proper places and cleared ship for Action, expecting another onset from them the first favourable opportunity that they could think of.

While this skirmish lasted, all the Bay and tops of the Hills round was full of Men, Women and children to behold the onset, and I dare say in great hopes of sharing all our nails and Toys, besides the pleasure of calling our great Canoe their own, and having all of us at their mercy, to ill or well use us as they thought most proper: but in place of that, when they came all running down to receive their Victorious friends, how terrible must they be shocked, to see their nearest and dearest of friends Dead, and torn to pieces in such a manner as I am certain they never beheld before. To Attempt to say what these poor Ignorant creatures thought of us, would be taking more upon me than I am able to perform.

Some of my mess-mates thought they would now look upon us as Demi-Gods, come to punish them for some of their past transgressions, but I think they were not yet fully confirmed in that opinion, altho' afterwards we had some reason to believe they were partly in that opinion, from some circumstances that happened soon after. Some on board now said they would certainly attack us again, in order to be revenged for the loss of their friends, and supposed the next onset would be in the night with fire-brands to set our ship on fire. This was not an unreasonable Conjecture as the Wind was always off shore at Night. There was some Reason for Guarding against this: in case of their making such an Attempt We therefore got our two three-pounders on the forecastle and put one of each side loaded with seventy musket Balls Each, and got fire-Grapnels all ready in the Boats, with all the Musquetoons loaded ready in the Boats, so that we Might not be surprised and taken at a disadvantage. Let them attempt what they will, we now thought we was able to give them such a reception as would soon put them to flight. At Noon there was not one canoe to be seen in the Water, nor ten people to be seen all along shore.

[The assault by the islanders, five days after the arrival of the *Dolphin*, was the crisis of the visit. Had it succeeded, the Western world might have waited long for news of Tahiti. As it did not, the safety of the ship's company was in fact assured, since the inhabitants had too much caution to risk another attack in full force.

A Journal of one of the Able Seamen, Francis Wilkinson of Chatham, supplements Robertson's account. He says the attack began with the islanders 'trying to weigh the stream anchor'. They were 'warned off by musket shots'. Shortly afterwards, he adds, 'we were surrounded with a Great Number of Indians in Canoes. It was observed that they had a Musical Instrument not unlike a German Flute, another not unlike a Drum.' (Captain Wallis says they 'blew conchs [shells] and played on flutes, and several with hoarse voices sang'.)

Wilkinson continues: 'They had Women amongst them, and Chiefs who seemed to have nothing to do but look on. Their Canoes were well stored with Fruit, Hogs, and Fowls for Traffic, but this was not their present business for the Women were Directed by the Men to stand in the Prow of their Canoes and Expose their Bodies Naked to our View. As our Men are in good Health and Spirits and begin to feel the Good Effect of the Fresh Pork, we Thank God for it. It is not to be wondered at that their Attention should be Drawn to a sight so uncommon to them, Especially as their Women are so well proportioned, their Features rather Agreeable than what is styled Beautiful, and tho' they are not so fair as our English Ladies I think they are infinitely too much so for their copper-coloured Husbands.

'In this posture they stood for a quarter of an Hour until they Judged our men were wholly exposed on the Gangways and

44

Booms and Forecastle, when upon a Signal given they began to throw Showers of stones with Great Rapidity. There were orders given to Fire upon them, and Accordingly we Fired great Guns, loaded with Grape and Round Shot. Their Retreat was as precipitate as their Attack was bold.

'Captain Wallis's Intention was to Frighten them more than hurt them. I believe they thought Themselves sure of the Ship, but our Fire arms spread an Inconceivable Terror through them, some jumping overboard, swimming to the Shore for their Lives. Their Stones struck some of our People, but did not disable Nobody.'

George Pinnock, one of the midshipmen, adds a final sad touch to the scene: 'Saw an Indian Woman floating athwart our cut-water, having received a Shot in her Belly.']

*25 June* THIS Day we had fine pleasant weather with a regular sea and Land breeze. We now set out with all our Boats and sounded the most part of the Bay, and found the whole fine Clear ground with gradual sounding. This gave us all great joy as we now found our ship in perhaps as fine a Bay as any in the world, besides we saw a river in the head of the Bay and the Water as smooth as a millpond, where we might land at any time we thought proper without wetting our feet, and have all our Arms dry to protect us from any insults of the Natives.

All night we had a fine pleasant land breeze, which brought off a fine agreeable smell, which made several of us suppose there was spices Growing here, either in the Low Grounds or on the high Mountains. For my own part I am partly in that Opinion still, that there is some sort of spices growing on the side of the mountains, but as I never got an opportunity to examine the mountain sides I cannot be certain—but I and several more on board has often viewed the sides of the Mountains at sunrise, and seen great numbers of trees bearing Flowers of various Colours which must certainly bear some sort of fruit yet unknown to us. But I shall drop this Discourse, as I know no more of the produce of the mountains nor a good spy-Glass discovered to me.

At Sun-rise we found all our new acquaintances had Employed themselves ashore, as there was not one canoe to be seen in the Water. We then unmoored and hove up and warped up towards the River, Where we moored in Nine fathom Water fine, soft sandy Ground, the best Bower to the NE and the small to the SW, with the stream laid out to the SE for a spring to keep our bows clear, and in case of blowing fresh to be ready to heave her broadside up, to make it bear on the watering place, in order to cover the people when filling the water.

Notwithstanding the skirmish that we had yesterday a few canoes ventured off about noon, with the tops of plantain Trees set up in the bows of their canoes, and small Branches in their hands, as Emblems of Peace and friendship. We this day behaved very haughty to them and only suffered two or three to come along-side at one time. When they disposed of what they had, We ordered them off, and let two or three more come along-side. The poor creatures used a great deal of ceremony this day. Before they came within a hundred yards of the ship, they all stood up and Looked hard at us and held up the plantain Boughs in their hands, and one of them made a long talk, and all the rest seemed very attentive until he had done. Then they all threw their Boughs to the sea, and began to

46

paddle nearer the ship, still keeping their eyes fixed on us, and if any of us looked surly they immediately held up the top of the plantain tree, and forced a sort of smile, then laid down the plantain tree top and showed us what they had got to sell. If we wanted what they brought off, we made signs for them to come along-side.

Then they began Another part of their ceremony, by pointing to the Green plantain Tree top, then made a long talk and put their bodies in several postures. Sometimes he who made the talk would look up to the Heavens seemingly very serious— then look at us and hold up the tree top for some time, then turn round and point to the shore. And to all his partners in the canoe, after that they again looked at us and talked a little, then threw the tree top on board the ship: then pointed to their Hogs, pigs, fowls and fruit and began to trade very fair and honestly.

But one of our seamen who was wounded in the head by some of the stones the day before, took an opportunity to Defraud one of the natives of two fowls, and when the poor fellow wanted to be paid he made a stroke at the man, in place of paying him for the two fowls. This the poor fellow resented by making a great noise and shaking his fist at the sailor, which was soon observed by some of our Young Gentlemen, who informed the Captain what had happened, and he immediately ordered the seaman to be punished with a Dozen of lashes, in order to deter others from Attempting to Defraud any of the Natives. The Captain Gave strict orders to punish every man that was found guilty of the like offence.

[Ben Butler's Journal records the delinquent seaman's name. It was Will Welsh. He got 24 lashes, not 12 as stated by Robertson. His end was sad. He peached on one of his shipmates, one Pinkney, later in the visit, and got him into trouble. Then, on 1 August, Robertson has the entry: 'At 6 a.m. Will Welsh, Seaman, in loosing the Main-sail, fell from the Main Yard upon the Starboard gangway, which occasioned his Death a few Hours afterwards.' He was a favourite with Robertson, as he had behaved bravely as a member of the

47

Jolly-Boat's crew on 23 June, the hour of Robertson's greatest personal danger—in his own view, at any rate. He 'showed the true Spirit of a British Tar', says Robertson.]

*26 June*  MODERATE fine pleasant weather, with regular sea and Land breezes. We now prepared for Landing at the Watering place, to take possession of this Beautiful Island in his Majesty's name. We first hove taut upon the spring and brought the ship's broadside to bear on the head of the Bay, then manned and armed the Barge, Cutter and Launch, and Quartered all the hands on board at the Great Guns, to be ready to fire upon the natives if they attempted to prevent our Boats from Landing.

When all this precaution was taken, Mr Furneaux the second Lieut. was ordered to take the command of the party, and to Land with the serjeant and twelve marines and Eighteen able seamen, besides three young Gentlemen to assist him, and Mr Molyneux, one of the mates, had the command of the three boats, with orders to bring them all three to anchor, with their Grapnels in a line along shore.

The Instant that the Lieut. landed he was to keep four men in Each boat ready to fire the musquetoons upon the natives, if they attacked our men; and if the party was obliged to retreat to the Boats, Mr Molyneux was to take care to keep the boats in about four foot of water, that the men might be able to Jump in. After all these orders were given the Boats set out, and in a few minutes Landed and formed on the Beach, and took possession of the Island In His Majesty's name, and Honoured it with the name of our Most Gracious sovereign King George the third.

Soon after they Landed about four or five hundred of the Natives assembled within musket shot of our men and began to advance slowly towards the River-side, every man carrying the bow of a Plantain Tree in his hand as an Emblem of Peace. When they got to the River-side they all stopped and made several friendly signs to our people, but none of them attempted

48

to cross the River until the Lieut. made a sign for some of them to come over. Then three Elderly Men set out directly and crossed the River, with a small pig in one hand and an Emblem of Peace in the other. When they got over the River the Lieut. made signs for one of the three to come up to him, and he Advanced about twenty yards from his party to meet the Old Man, who came up with his Emblem of Peace and the Young Pig by way of a Peace Offering.

When the Old Man came within a few Yards of the Lieut. he made a full stop, and talked for some time, then laid down the pig and laid the plantain bough on the top of it. Then the Lieut. made a short talk to the Old Man and ordered one of the seamen to receive the peace-offering, and the Lieut. paid the Old Man with Nails and Toys, and let him know that we wanted Water, which he made signs for us to take as much as we wanted. Then the Lieut. Ordered our men to roll two small casks in to the River, and fill them, which was immediately done, at same time he ordered some men to fix a long pole in the Ground, and hoisted a pendant on it in token of our having taken Possession of that place.

While this was doing several of the natives brought over small Hogs and pigs and some fruit, and laid them down with an Emblem of Peace with Each, and immediately returned back to their friends on the other side of the River and waited there until the Lieut. ordered our men to carry all on board the Boats, and laid down toys, Nails and two Bill-hooks for the Hogs, pigs and fruit: which the Old man came over and took up, and the Lieut. and him shook hands and parted very Good friends. Then our Boats returned On board with the Hogs, pigs, fruit and two casks of as good water as ever was drunk, and informed us that we could water here with the Greatest Ease imaginable. The sandy beach is as smooth as a Mill-pond, and the side of the River is not above twenty yards from the Beach, so that this is a most Excellent place to water at.

We now thought ourselves very happy, and made very little doubt of getting all sorts of refreshments soon. When the

Natives saw our boats return, great numbers of them came over the River to the place where our men stood, and every man brought over a plantain Branch in his hand, and viewed the place all round, but was a considerable time before they ventured near the pendant; they all seemed Afraid of it, not knowing what it was put there for.

At last a few of them began to approach towards the pendant; I then had the curiosity to view them with a very good spy-Glass, and saw two Old Men advance first, with two large plantain tree tops in their hands. They seemed to approach it with as much ceremony as if it had been a Demi-God. They made a stop at every Eight or ten paces, and seemed to talk some time, looking up very attentively to the pendant, which was hoisted on a very long spar. When they got within about two or three yards of the foot of the pendant the two Old Men fell down on their knees and seemingly made a long prayer, then laid down the Green boughs at the foot of the pendant and Marched back to where the rest stood.

After that some hundreds of them Went up to the Pendant in Much the same manner as the first two old men, and they all carried green boughs which they laid down at the foot of the pendant. At one time I saw about twenty of them all on their knees together; when they knelt down it happened to be calm, and the pendant hung right up and down. A few minutes after there sprung up a fresh breeze, which blew the pendant out, and the end of it came right over their heads; this frightened them so much that they all started back and run some distance. Before they ventured to look Back they were about fifty yards off, and I dare say they were so much Afraid at the shake of the pendant, as if a Great Gun had been fired at them.

After this several of them carried Green boughs and laid down, but none of them knelt down to it any more. A little before sunset I saw two men carrying two large Hogs towards the pendant. When they came near it they laid down the Hogs and stood a few minutes, then laid down a Green Bough each at the foot of the pendant, and returned Back and took the two Hogs up and Laid them down at the foot of the pendant, and

50

stood some time before they took them up, sometimes looking at the ship then at their friends.

I suppose they were making some long talk in order to make peace with us. When the ceremony was over the two men carried the two Hogs into a canoe and brought them off to the ship. Their canoe was almost full of Green boughs, and they both made a long speech and threw some Green Boughs into the sea, and some they threw on board the ship, then made signs for a rope to haul the two Hogs on board.

When we got in the two fine fat Hogs of about fifty pound Each, we offered them Toys for them and some nails, but they would receive nothing from us—but still kept talking and pointing to the pendant meaning, as we afterwards found, to give the Hogs for liberty to strike the pendant. While these two old men was along-side, some of our people observed two men throw some stones at the Pendant, and drive off all their country-men from it, that was laying down plantain tree boughs, and using the same ceremony as the others did, but this I saw not; however, the very instant that the old men Landed they went and struck the pendant and carried it clear off.[1]

All this night we had fine pleasant weather with some refreshing showers: we heard no noise all this night, but saw several large fires on the sides of the Hills along shore—which I suppose was a signal to call the people of the country together. From the River to the SW end of the Island there was several very great fires.

At daylight we Manned and Armed all the Boats the same as yesterday, and carried a few water-casks ashore to fill with some spare hands, besides the thirty armed men. In two hours time we got off three Tun of exceeding good water, and filled about three tuns more, which we intended to bring off. But at $\frac{1}{2}$ past 7 A.M. we observed a great number of large canoes,

[1] This pendant was taken later by the local Queen, Oberea, and converted into a sacred girdle. Cook saw it in 1777 'ornamented with red, yellow and black feathers'. Five years earlier, Spanish visitors to Tahiti had noted instant recognition of an English flag which was in their ship's signal-lockers.

coming towards the ship from the SW side of the Bay, and all full of men, at the same time we saw several thousands of Men coming along-shore toward the River. The first great body of men came over the top of a Hill in the Bottom of the Bay, with our pendant flying at the end of a long pole, amongst the middle of them.

He that carried the pendant appeared to be a tall brisk young man and the most of them appeared to be Armed with spears and sticks or some such thing. This sight alarmed us all and we soon Expected another skirmish, therefore the Captain Ordered the Jolly-Boat to go and order off Mr Furneaux with all our men from the shore. By the time our men embarked there was several hundreds of the Natives within Gun-shot of them, and several thousands coming through the woods towards the watering place. There was a great many of them that had no sort of arms, but we supposed they were for throwing stones, as we saw great numbers of stones piled up like shot all along the River-side.

When our men were fairly embarked the Captain gave orders to fire a few random shot into the Woods, in order to frighten them and make them disperse: but this had not the Desired Effect, until we was obliged to fire a few round and Grape shot amongst the thickest of them. Then they began to run to the top of the Hill, where they supposed they were safe. This we called Skirmish Hill. By this time about a hundred large canoes lay by abreast of the north end of Skirmish Hill, and sent some of their party ashore to get information how those on shore went on.

We observed some of them return from the shore and hold some sort of counsel. Soon after they began to paddle towards us, but at a very slow rate; we supposed they were waiting a great number more canoes which was paddling up from the SW point of the Bay to join them, before they attacked us. When we observed their intention we let them come within a short mile of us, then fired a round shot amongst them in hopes they would give over their Design—but they still persisted, as the shot hurt none of them. We therefore fired some

52

round and Grape shot amongst them: this soon put them to flight, and the most of them ran their canoes ashore, and ran into the Woods thinking themselves safe there, but we soon convinced them that the woods was not able to protect them from our round and Double-headed shot, as the shot brought down several of the trees, and great numbers of the Branches about their Heads, which they afterwards showed us when we became good friends.

This so terrified them that they all fled to the top of Skirmish Hill; there a great number of them sat down and thought themselves very safe, and all the canoes that was coming up from the SW end of the Bay put ashore, but about five or six which pulled close in-shore until they got amongst those who put Ashore at the N end of Skirmish Hill. We then fired one Gun Loaded with round and Grape shot at them, that soon sent them after their friends to the top of the Hill.

By that time there was upward of seventy or Eighty large canoes at the North End of Skirmish Hill capable of carrying from Eight to ten hundred men, and all ready to Launch off in a minute's warning, when the dark night comes on; this we supposed might be their plan, as so many of them kept on the top of the Hill close by the Canoes. Therefore, to prevent their attempting any such plan, the Captain gave orders to man and arm all the Boats, and to carry Ashore all the Carpenters and those who could use an axe to destroy all the Canoes which lay at or near the N end of Skirmish Hill.

This Order was soon complied with and our Boats Landed all the Carpenters with several other hands, and began to cut the canoes in the middle. In about two or three hours our people rendered about Eighty Canoes incapable of swimming, several of them from forty to fifty foot long and capable of carrying upwards of thirty men. This a few of the Natives observed and went and informed the rest, and several of them ventured down through the wood, I suppose with an intention to prevent our men from disabling their canoes; but the Guard which landed to protect the carpenters, fired upon them and soon put them to the flight, and obliged them to Retire to the top of Skirmish Hill, where they still thought they were safe, until we threw a round shot close by them which rose the Earth that they could not help looking at the hole it made.

After that they all Retired to the back of the Hill and never Attempted to Molest us any more. I really Believe the shot which fell close by them on the top of the Hill, frightened them more than anything which we did; indeed none of us supposed that any of our shot would have gone so far, we only tried it for Experiment's sake. The first shot that we fired at the top of the Hill fell short about ¼ mile, but the second fell within ten or fifteen yards of the crowd on the top of the Hill —this shot I suppose made them think they were in danger of being shot anywhere in sight of the ship.

This day the Captain gave orders, to let every man in the ship have as many cocoa-nuts, and other fruit as they thought proper to Eat, likewise ordered Hogs and Pigs to be killed to make broth for all hands, besides several of the men had fine fowls which they purchased before: in short all hands now lived so well that they began to revive their sunk spirits, and most of the sick began to crawl upon deck.

[On this day the Captain, wishing to reinforce the lesson of the defeated attack, caused a pistol to be fired through the prows of one of the canoes, which, says John Nichols, whose Journal records the incident, caused an impression. Of the destruction of the canoes he noted: 'two in particular were of a larger size than common, with very pretty carved work on them, much resembling the Doric Order of Architecture. They measure 50 feet in length and a foot and a half in breadth.'

Wilkinson adds that the Indians this day 'traded with a great deal of Submission and Honesty . . . we Endeavoured to make them Understand that Honesty is the Best Policy'. The Captain apparently gave them a 'round shot and a bag of grape' to make them realize precisely what had caused their losses.]

THIS day we had fine pleasant weather with a regular sea breeze all Day, and a land breeze at night the very same as in Jamaica, only the sea breeze was not near so strong. We likewise had some fine refreshing showers.

The instant that our Boat returned from disabling all the canoes at the N end of Skirmish Hill, we saw a large body of Men and Women Assembling on the beach to the Northward of the Watering place, and Bringing down Green boughs with Hogs, pigs, fowls and fruits, and a great quantity of White cloth. We supposed these people wanted to make peace with us, and what they were bringing down was intended for a peace-offering to prevent us from destroying their canoes as we did those to the southward of the watering place.

Immediately after dinner the second Lieut. took the Barge and Cutter Manned and Armed and the Launch Loaded with Empty Water Casks. He first brought the Launch to an Anchor off the Watering place, then Landed where the Peace-Offering was laid down, and walked a few steps towards the place where their canoes was hauled up on the Beach, as if he meant to destroy them as he did those to the southward.

When the natives saw him going towards the canoes they seemed Greatly afraid, and made all the signs of friendliness that they could think of, and pointed to the peace-offering, which consisted of Eight large Hogs, four pigs, a Dozen fowls, some fruit and six large Bales of the Country cloth, from six to Eight yards in Each bale—besides two fine fat Dogs [1] with their fore feet tied on their backs. All this they made signs for our people to take; then the Lieut. Ordered the men to take the Hogs, pigs, fowls and fruit, and put them in the boat, but cast loose the two poor dogs who run a mile before they stopped to look back at their deliverers; but the cloth he made signs for the natives to take Back, as it was of very little use to us and certainly a great loss to them; but they seemed greatly afraid when they saw he left the cloth, and made signs for him to take it away, but he thought it better to let it alone and

[1] Dogs were bred for food in Tahiti.

Laid down hatchets, Bill-hooks, nails and some toys, and made signs for the Natives to take these things and their cloth, but none of them would come near or accept of any thing.

Because the cloth was not received by our people they thought the peace was not concluded, but the Lieut. not thinking that was their reason, went to the watering place and sent off about six tun, then all returned On board without being molested by any of the Natives, but still observed the poor people to the NE of the watering place bringing down Green boughs, and waving them round their heads: we therefore Judged the Reason, and sent the two Armed boats for the cloth. The instant our men laid hold of the cloth, there appeared Joy in every one of the Natives' faces. When the cloth was put in the Boats our people made signs for the Natives to take the things which we laid down. This they complied with and Brought down some more Hogs, pigs and fruit. This our men received and paid them with nails and toys.

But our Young men seeing several very handsome Young girls, they could not help feasting their Eyes with so agreeable a sight. This was observed by some of the Elderly men, and several of the Young Girls was drawn out, some a light copper colour, others a mulatto, and some almost White. The old men made them stand in Rank, and made signs for our people to take which they liked best, and as many as they liked: and for fear our men had been Ignorant and not known how to use the poor young Girls, the old men made signs how we should behave to the Young women. This all the boat's crew seemed to understand perfectly well, and begged the Officer would receive a few of the Young Women on board; at same time they made signs to the Young Girls, that they were not so Ignorant as the old men supposed them. This seemed to please the Old men Greatly, when they saw our people merry, but the poor young Girls seemed a little afraid, but soon after turned better acquainted.

The Officer in the boat having no orders to bring off any of the natives, would not receive the Young Girls, but made signs that he would see them afterwards, and Ordered all our men on board the Boats, and returned on board the Ship. When our boats returned to the ship all the sailors swore they never saw handsomer made women in their lives, and declared they would all to a man, live on two-thirds allowance, rather nor lose so fine an opportunity of getting a Girl apiece. This piece of news made all our men madly fond of the shore, even the sick which had been on the Doctor's list for some weeks before, now declared they would be happy if they were permitted to go ashore, and at same time said a Young Girl would make an Excellent Nurse, and they were Certain of recovering faster under a Young Girl's care nor all the Doctor would do for them. We passed this Night very merry, supposing all hostilities was now over, and to our great joy it so happened.

At sunrise we manned and Armed the Boats, and got off about three tun of Water. While our men was Ashore a few of the Natives to the NE brought down large bundles of Plantains, Bananas, Bread Fruit and a fine large sort of fruit which we called Apples,[1] because they looked the likest to apples of any fruit that we could think of. This perhaps is the finest fruit in the world, they are the best fruit to Eat off the Trees that I ever saw, and they made most excellent pies, tarts and puddings, that ever was Eat, but in my opinion they rather ought to be called peaches nor apples, because they have a large stone in Each, and the make of them is more like a peach, but a great deal larger and better Eating. The plantains and Bananas is much larger and finer Eating, nor any that I ever saw in Jamaica. As for their Bread-fruit, I look upon them to be the best substitute for Bread when properly dressed.

We had now so many Hogs and pigs on board, that the Captain desired fresh pork broth to be made for all hands every day while they lasted, and great plenty of Bread-fruit, cut down plantains and Bananas, and boiled amongst the Broth. This made the most excellent food I ever saw, for recovering the strength and spirits of poor distressed seamen, after living so long upon salt provisions as our men had done. We now

[1] The vi-apple (*spondias dulcis*): green with a golden lustre, speckled with brownish dots.

Employed the carpenters in repairing the defects of the ship, and some hands painting her. The sailmakers was all Employed repairing her sails, and the seamen repairing the Rigging.

*28 June* THIS day we had fine pleasant weather with regular sea and Land breeze. Loosed all our sails and dried them, and kept the people repairing all the Rigging, sails etc. From three to six P.M. we saw a very Great Number of the Natives fishing, upon a great Reef, which lies off the SW point of the Bay, but know now what sort of fish they catch. None of the canoes came off to trade with us this day—but several of the Natives ventured to carry off the Great double canoes, which we cut down at the last skirmish.

The method that they took was this; first one man stole down and Launched a single canoe and paddled her close alongshore, still keeping his Eye upon the ship for fear of being fired at. When this poor fellow got clear off, without our seeming to take notice of him, about ten of them crawled down to the Beach upon their hands and feet, and Launched off one of the double canoes. The instant she was afloat two stout fellows Jumped on board of her and Paddled off to the southward as fast as they were able, and the rest ran into the woods as fast as they could run. In this manner they carried off all that was not fairly cut in two Except two which we brought on board and cut up for fire-wood. It was once resolved to take the whole for fire-wood, but we thought that would be too cruel, and would distress the poor people too much. We therefore let them carry the rest all off without any trouble from us.

This night we saw a great number of lights on the SW Reef. I suppose they were fishing. At Sunrise we manned and Armed the Boats and got off about three tuns of Water. While the Launch crew was filling the Water, and getting it off, Eight Marines and Eight seamen stood on the River-side all under arms to protect the Waterers, at same time about two hundred of the Natives came down to the other side of the River and brought down a good many fowls and several large bundles of fruits and made signs that they wanted to trade with our men.

The Gunner being Commanding Officer made Signs for one of them to bring the fowls and fruit over, but they were a long time before any of them would venture, and the whole of them kept staring at the men under Arms, and seemed Greatly Afraid until the men grounded their Arms. Then several of them ventured into the river, but the Gunner only allowed one old man to bring a fowl and some fruit over and waved the others back. The old man delivered the fowl and fruit, and Mr Harrison the Gunner gave him a tenpenny nail for the fowl, and a sixpenny nail for the Bundle of Fruit. This pleased the old man and he went for a few more fowls and some bundles of fruit. At Noon the Boats were always ordered to come off to Dinner, so that we got but few fowls this day, and but very little fruit, as Mr Harrison allowed none but the old man to bring any trade over the River. He was not able to bring a tenth part of what they had in the time, and when our boats came off all the Natives dispersed and went off I suppose to their Dinner.

This Day the Captain gave strict Orders to the Gunner not to let any of our men go across the River, nor to allow above two or three of the Natives to come on our side, neither was he to allow any of the men to trade with the Natives, but to carry on all the trade himself. This made our trade go on but slowly, and prevented discoveries of all kinds for some time. Except one discovery which John Woolridge made this day by accident; when he was filling the water he found a large piece of Salt-petre which he delivered to Mr Furneaux when he came on board; how this piece of Salt-petre came here I know not, but I think there is certainly more in this country.

There was a good many women came down to the waterside, but none of them would venture across the River; our Men say they saw trinkets of some kind in all their Ears, but being at a good distance from them, they could not tell what the Ear-rings was made of. This piece of News gave us some hopes of finding something of very great value when we could venture into the country to make proper discoveries. At this time our

Captain and first Lieut. was both very bad and for most part confined to their Beds. I believe this made the Captain give the above orders to the Gunner, and it was supposed the Gunner was the Man that persuaded the Captain to give this order, out of a private view, that he might have it in his power to carry on all the trade, as we had now resolved to let no canoe trade along-side the ship, but to send every Day the Gunner with fourteen or sixteen Armed men, besides four of the Young Gentlemen and the serjeant of Marines to assist him.

*29 June*  THIS day we had a fine brisk Gale Easterly, with Clear weather. The first part of the day we was Employed painting the ship, repairing the sails and Rigging etc. At Night we had fine pleasant weather and saw great numbers of Lights on the SW reef—and several on the Reef that lies off the N end of the bay. At Sunrise we manned and Armed the Boats, and the Gunner and his party went trading and the waterers brought off about three tun of water.

At noon the trading party returned On board, and brought off about twenty small pigs, a dozen fowl, and a great Quantity of Good fruit. None of the Natives was suffered to cross the water this day but the old man who brought over the trade yesterday and a young fellow which was supposed to be his son. There was a great number of the natives assembled at the Watering this day and several attempted to come over to trade for that they brought down, but they were not permitted; but the Gunner took care to secure the old man and his son in his Interest, by making them some presents. This I think was a very prudent precaution, but some of the young Gentlemen who were on the spot thought otherwise. They say this gave Umbrage to the other people of the Island, particularly to some who had the Appearance of the first rank, and this old man was only one of the middle rank, and seemed to pay a great deal of respect to some of the others, who seemed to have servants with them, and great plenty of stock, but would send none of it over by the old man, because they were not permitted to come themselves. There was nothing curious found this day, nor no pains taken to find anything but Hogs, fowls and fruit.

[At this point Captain Wallis notes that the Purser, Mr. Harrison, had joined the sick-list. He reports that while the 'scorbutic men' recover fast, 'bilious fevers and colics continue', including his own and that of the First Lieutenant, who had apparently been bad 'near six weeks'. The Purser's illness was a short one. By 5 July he was 'better'.]

*30 June* WE had fine pleasant weather with some refreshing showers, and a regular sea and Land breeze. I this day observed the Latitude of this place and found it to be 17°: 30 South. The first part of the day we was Employed repairing the Sails and Rigging etc.—At night we had fine pleasant weather and saw several large fires upon the land, but none upon either of the Reefs. This made us a little suspicious of their making signals for another skirmish, but found nothing like any bad intention amongst them next morning.

When the trading and watering parties went ashore, and carried Ashore a tent for the coopers to set up some water casks, and a sail to make a shed for the Guard to shelter themselves from the Sun, they traded very peaceably this day, and no murmuring was made, as the Gunner allowed several of the natives to cross the River to sell their own goods. One man Brought over a curious kind of thing in his hand, made up of several pieces of Shells. We afterwards found out that they used this thing as a decoy, to bring the fish within their reach to stick or throw a net over them, and sometimes they use it when angling: one decoys the fish and the other catches them with a very fine small mother-of-pearl hook.—The Gunner purchased this decoy, and some Mother-of-pearl Hooks; this plainly told us, that there must be a pearl fishery about this Island, or not far from it, likeways

plenty of very fine shells; so much for the discoveries of this day. All our people has fine fresh pork and good Broth every day for dinner, and wheat boiled for Breakfast, with four pound of portable soup and plenty of Bread fruit, plantains and Bananas in it. This makes a most Excellent Meal, and all the Sick men recover fast.

We now begin to think the Natives will be peaceable, and the Doctor told the Captain that the sick ought now to go Ashore every day for the recovery of their health. This the Captain agreed to, and ordered a sail to be carried ashore to shelter the sick men from the Sun; at same time he gave strict orders, that no man should straggle away into the woods, for fear of accidents.

*1 July* WE had fine pleasant weather with some refreshing showers and a regular sea and land breeze; the first part of the day Employed Repairing the Sails and Rigging, and finished painting the Ship. At Night we had fine pleasant weather with refreshing Showers, which brought off a very agreeable smell from the land.

At sunrise the traders and waterers went ashore, and about twenty liberty men, the most of them on the sick list, but all able to walk about a Little. The sick tent was pitched upon a small island in the middle of the River, and the Sick was carried through the smallest branch of the River to the tent, and all those who was able had a Cutlass to defend themselves with, and two of the young Gentlemen with four Marines Stood Guard over the sick tent, to prevent the people from strolling away from the Island.

At Noon the Trading party and all the liberty men returned On board, and brought off Nine Hogs and Pigs, Eight fowls and some fruit, which was all paid for with Nails, buttons and Beads. Several of the Natives came over to our people and traded very fair and honest and seemed to be very friendly. Some of the Young Girls came over and Traded with the Gunner for their Earrings which was pearls of a fine lustre, but all spoiled in the boring. How they are able to bore pearls I know not, but I think it's Impossible to do it without some small metal Instrument, as no bone or shell can pierce a pearl, neither can any kind of stone be brought to so fine a point as to bore so small a hole as was in these pearls, for which reason I am almost certain they have some kind of metal, but what kind it is I never was able to discover.[1]

2 July WE had moderate cloudy weather with some Lightning and Rain, and the wind Variable all round the Compass, and sometimes calm. The first part of the day we was Employed repairing all our sails and Rigging. At night we had frequent showers with Lightning: saw no Lights on either of the Reefs neither saw we any upon the Shore, which makes me suppose all the Natives kept close quarters this night.

At sunrise the trading party, Waterers and twenty Liberty men all went ashore. All the Liberty men went to the Island, and the traders to their usual place where some hundreds of the natives was ready to trade with them, but the Gunner thought them too numerous, therefore permitted none but the old man and his son to carry on the trade betwixt the Natives and us. This precaution in some respects was very necessary, but at the same time it disgusted the people, who brought down several very fine fat Hogs, pigs and fowls and the most of them returned home with their stocks, so that we only got off four young pigs and two hogs and some fruit. Several of the natives wanted to come over to the Liberty men to trade with them, but were not permitted. At noon all hands returned on board to Dinner, and After dinner our first Lieut. being pretty well recovered he went with a party of men to haul the seine,[2] but caught no fish. At this time Capt. Wallis was Extremely bad,

[1] Whatever was done to the pearls Robertson saw was in fact done by stone, bone or shell. Captain Wallis remarks that even the adzes with which the Tahitians built their canoes were of stone.

[2] *Seine:* large fish-net, of a type French in origin.

and the Surgeon was very much afraid of his Life, but all our Seamen was recovering very fast.

[George Pinnock, a midshipman with some talent for drawing, records under this date that Richard Kean, a seaman, had a dozen lashes 'for disobeying orders whilst ashore'.]

*3 July*  WE had frequent hard squally showers of Wind and Rain, and the Wind Variable. Got the shore cable bent and the Anchor over the side. This was a dark dismal squally night with a great deal of Lightning, but not much wind to endanger either ship or boat. At Sunrise the weather cleared up with a fine fresh breeze Easterly. Sent all our traders, waterers and Liberty men Ashore, and scrubbed the Ship betwixt wind and Water, and packed the bins with warm tar.[1] Our copper bottom looked as well as the first day we came out of England. At Noon our people all returned on board and brought off one hog and six small pigs. There was a great number of the Natives came down this day, but they brought but very little stock down with them; this was owing to the indifferent treatment which they got the day before.

One of the young Gentlemen that was along with the Guard told me that a great many of the principal people of the Island came down to the River-side with servants attending them, carrying stools for their masters and mistresses to sit down on along the River-side. Several of them brought down Large Hogs to trade with us for Nails and other things which they wanted, but the Gunner would permit none of them to Cross the river but the old man and his son. When any of the others set their foot in to cross the River, he ordered some of the Guard to point their muskets at them, which frightened them greatly and made them return back trembling to their own side, and very often go off into the Woods and not return again.

The poor Creatures now knew the use of fire-arms by

[1] Bins, with lids on top, usually made of deal. Packing the outsides with warm tar was to help keep the contents waterproof.

64

Experience, therefore was greatly terrified when a musket was pointed at them. This Gentleman says the Gunner was at all the pains imaginable to make the old man and his son get him some pearls from the women, but they seeing themselves treated like slaves, and not permitted to come over to trade themselves for what they wanted, the most of them took all their pearls or what other trinkets they had out of their Ears, and showed them in their Ears no more.

[Henry Ibbott's Journal has a significant entry under this day. 'The Women', he says, 'were far from being coy. For when a Man found a girl to his mind, which he might easily do Amongst so many, there was not much Ceremony on either side, and I believe whoever comes here after will find Evident Proofs that they are not the first Discoverers. The Men are so far from having Objection to Intercourse of this kind that they Brought down their Women and Recommended them to us with the greatest Eagerness, which makes me Imagine they want a Breed of English men Amongst them.']

*4 July* W E had fine pleasant clear weather with fine regular Sea and Land breezes. The first part of this day we was Employed Completing our Rigging and overhauling our Sea provisions, and making a thorough clean all over the ship. We now got up our yards and top-masts and tarred all our yards and standing rigging. At Night we had a fine pleasant land breeze which never failed to bring off a sweet and agreeable smell of various sorts of fruits and herbs.

At Sunrise we sent all the boats ashore with the traders, waterers and Liberty men. This day the traders brought off only four pigs, some fowls and a little fruit. There still was a great number of the natives at the River-side but none of them permitted to come over to trade, but the favourite old man and his son, which seemed to disoblige the other people Greatly.

All the Young Gentlemen said they had observed for some days past that none of the Natives brought down any kind of

Offensive weapons, not so much as a stick in their hand; this plainly tells they meant to be friends with us. We this day ordered all the liberty men that was able to cut grass, to make hay for our sheep, there being great plenty of very fine Grass on the Island. This was a very good Moderate Exercise for the sick and gave them a little more liberty to walk about in order to find proper Grass for cutting; before, they were never Suffered to go to the nearest end of the Island, but this day they strolled about a good way, and all returned on board greatly refreshed, and the whole of the men say all the natives appear to be very peaceable and friendly inclined. Several of them wanted to come over to the liberty men with Hogs, fowls and fruit, but none was permitted.

This Day our people was served Salt provisions, there not being a sufficient quantity of fresh pork On board. This was entirely owing to the treatment we gave the Natives, who it's reasonable to think had some Sense of Good and bad ways as well as we.

I this day Enquired of Mr Harrison the Gunner, his reason for not permitting more of the natives to come over, and trade with him themselves for what they wanted, Especially as they seemed all peaceable and friendly Inclined, and none of them brought any Offensive or defensive weapons with them. His Answer was he believed there was no kind of danger in trusting them to come to his side, but Mr Clarke gave him strict orders to let none of them come over, but the favourite old man and his son, for fear of being surprised with them, as he supposed them to be a treacherous people and always ready and willing to take the advantage. He likeways ordered him not to let any of the Liberty men go out of his sight, nor yet to permit any of the young Gentlemen to trade for anything. This in my Opinion was behaving very ungenteel to all the Young Gentlemen, several of them having passed for Officers, and the rest all young Gentlemen ready and willing to learn the Duty of a seaman and Officer.

I do not mention this as a reflection on the Gunner; the man was very capable of doing his own duty as a Gunner, but

in my Opinion, not at all capable of Commanding Gentlemen, who has no other view of coming into the Navy, but to
be made Officers. I cannot help thinking a Gunner a very
improper person to Command any Gentleman that has served
his time in the Navy upon the King's Quarter-Deck, and has
passed a regular Examination before the Honourable Commissioners of His Majesty's Navy, and by them qualified for an
Officer. This is rather foreign from my present purpose, but
a few words which passed between me and another Officer in
the Ship, makes me mention this here, that I may have the
Opportunity of some time knowing the Opinion of other
Gentlemen in the Navy on this head.

['I must say', runs an entry in Ibbott's Journal for this day,
'that the girls which were of the white sort would admit of
any freedom but the last, which they would not, every one
having, by what I saw, a Man or Husband. Petticoat interest
here as well as in other parts is the most prevailing, the principal person hereabout who appeared to have any authority
being a Woman whom we Styled the Queen. She was the
stoutest woman I ever saw there and had a very commanding
aspect.'
Wilkinson says the Queen was partial to the Serjeant of
Marines. Events showed that he was not her only favourite.]

*5 July*  WE had fine Moderate Cloudy weather with a
regular sea and Land breeze. This day we caught a large She-
Shark which Measured twelve foot six inches. After she took
the hook we was obliged to shoot her in the head several times,
and some of the men run one of the Gunner's pricks into her
belly several times before she was quite Dead. After she was
dead we towed her ashore to the Watering-place in order to
show her to the natives, and Ordered the boat to come off
Directly after landing the Shark, that we might have an
Opportunity of seeing how they would behave with the Shark.
Before night came on—the instant that they saw our boat put

off, the Natives assembled in a great body near where the Shark was lying.

I had the curiosity to view their manner of proceeding with a very good Spy-Glass. They made the first stop at about twenty yards distance, then advanced at a very slow pace until they came within about ten yards of her, then stopped a long time, until several of them went up for Green boughs to make peace with this Sea Monster. When they came down with the Green boughs, two of them stepped up to the dead creature very slowly, and laid down the Green boughs at its head and started back some paces, where they stood some minutes, and made some sort of speech and looked very steadfastly on the dead shark. I suppose they still thought it Living and were afraid to come near it, until they were certain of its being Dead.

When the two men had done with their talk or prayer or whatever it was, they again stepped up slowly to the creature, and several of the rest came up with Green boughs, and laid them down by the creature. This ceremony of making peace with this Sea Monster continued near an hour. By that time I suppose they were fully convinced that the creature was dead, then one of them ventured to put his foot upon the tail of the Shark, and not seeing it move he ventured to lay hold of the tail and gave it a great pull, then Another man began to look narrowly at its head and thrust his fingers into the shot holes. Then they all stood still a few minutes and looked at the Ship, I suppose wondering how it was possible for us to kill so great a Monster.

We then sent a boat Ashore and made Signs for them to carry it off. This they complied with and in about fifteen minutes they cut it all up in large pieces and carried it off, and I dare say dressed and Eat it that night. They appeared all very cheerful when we allowed them to carry it off. Our men say there was about twenty Young Sharks in the Belly of the old one.

This night we had fine pleasant weather with a brisk land Wind. We saw a great many Lights on both Reefs, but never saw any of their canoes in the night-time. At Sunrise we sent

68

our traders, Waterers and Liberty men ashore as usual, and the Gunner allowed the people to bring their stock to Market themselves, but the instant he paid for them he made them return back. By this means he brought off Eight Hogs, four pigs, Eighteen fat fowls and great plenty of fruit. All the Natives seemed very cheerful and Merry, and some of the Young Girls brought fowls to market, which was paid with ten-penny nails, but to encourage trade the Young Gentlemen gave them some Earrings and the Gunner gave them beads, which he tied about their neck and wrists. This pleased the Young Girls much, and made trade go on well.

This day some of the Young Girls ventured over to the Liberty men, and our honest-hearted tars received them with great cheerfulness, and made them some little presents which gained the hearts of the Young Girls, and made them give our men a signal, which they would have willingly obeyed, had they not been immediately ordered on board. We this day served fresh pork, and made Excellent good broth of the fine fat hogs and fruit.

[Ben Butler records that on this day the Captain 'punished Walter Bowman with 12 lashes for insolence and disobeying commands'. Furneaux adds that he 'struck the Coxswain of the Barge'.]

*6 July* WE had fine clear pleasant weather with a regular sea and Land breeze. At sunset we saw several thousands of People on the SW reef and a good many on the N reef all fishing. At Night we had fine pleasant weather with some refreshing showers, but saw no lights on either reef nor none on the shore. At sunrise sent our traders, Waterers and Liberty men ashore. At same time the Captain being greatly recovered chose to take an Airing round the bay in his Barge, and I went along with him and took all the different bearings of the most remarkable places, and sounded all the S side of the bay which we had not an opportunity of sounding before.

When we set out there was several small canoes without the reef fishing, but on seeing us sailing round the Bay they all pulled Ashore, and only one of the whole would come near us, who speared us a few fish for some trinkets. When we got to a point bearing about SW from the Ship two miles, we there struck our mast and sail, and lay some time viewing a great number of people on the Reef fishing, and several large canoes close by them. We not having more than one boat, and knowing that their canoes sailed much faster than our boats, thought it was too great a risk to go near the Reef, to see what sort of fish they was catching there, for fear the poor Creatures should be foolish enough to Attack us, and put us under the disagreeable necessity of killing a few of them.

We therefore determined to row back to the Ship—but to keep close in-shore to get a full view of the coast. Here we saw two very large double Canoes about fifty foot Long, which I dare say would have carried near Eight ton. They were upon the top of a reef of Rocks, and raised about two foot, with several large Logs of Wood under them. They appeared to be raised for dressing their Bottoms. After the same manner that we would raise a ship to put on a new keel.

After this we rowed close along-shore, and saw a most curious place all built up with round sort of stones, the Outermost part of this building was close on the sea side, and about six foot high, and about Eight foot broad on the top, then another Wall of about four foot high and near the same breadth on the top, and within that another wall of about three foot high and very broad at the top of all. The front of this building was near fifty yards Long, and about fifteen or sixteen yards Broad, the side that faced the Land had seven regular steps about two foot high Each; by these steps it was an easy matter to ascend to the top.

We supposed this to be some place of Worship,[1] with the appearance of several burying-places close by it, and some Images rudely carved out of large trees, and set up close by the

[1] The Tahitians usually built their altars and burial-places on promontories. They did not cremate their dead, but buried, exposed or mummified them.

building, which I suppose is an Altar, where they erect funeral piles to burn the bodies of their Dead, but this is only conjecture; but I remember to see several large smokes here at different times. There was a large reef of rocks round this place, which prevented us from rowing close to it with the boat, and it was thought dangerous to Land, and walk round to view it as there was great Numbers of the natives Assembling on the Beach, but none of them went near this place, they all kept

a good way off. When they came round to view us, I often wished to have a full view of this place, but never after got an opportunity.

As we rowed along we still kept sounding, and found plenty of Water and clear good ground for any ship to Anchor in. We likewise saw several very fine runs of Water, and good Landing for boats or canoes in every little Bay. We also saw great numbers of Hogs and Young Pigs running all along shore, and great plenty of Fowls and fruit of all sorts. The Hogs here appear to be a Chinese breed, none of them above Eighty or a hundred pound weight, and the fowls are the same as ours in England. How Either come to be transported here I know not, unless the high Mountains which we saw to the Southward of this place, be a part of what is called New Zealand, which I am apt to think it is. In that case both might reasonably be supposed to have first come from the continent, to Sumatra, Java, and New Holland and in time from that to New Zealand and from thence here—and I think it is Reasonable to suppose the people of this Island has in time come from the same quarter of the World.

There is three distinct colours of people here,[1] which is a thing most difficult to account for of anything which we have yet seen; the Red people are ten times more numerous nor the Mustees,[2] which is a Medium between the Whitest sort and the red or Indian Colour, and the Mustees are near ten times as numerous as the Whitest sort.

At the south end of Skirmish hill we lay some time on our Oars, and traded for some good fat fowls, some fish and several very fine bunches of Plantains and Bananas, and paid all with small trinkets, such as Beads, buttons etc. While we lay trading a great Number of Men, Women and Children came down to the beach, and the Captain sent several strings of beads to the Young Children, which pleased the old people very much. Here we saw two places walled in like a Garden, and a nursery of young trees in it. The Wall was made of Stone and about three foot high, which was sufficient to keep out the Hogs which is the most dangerous Creature that we saw for spoiling Gardens or Nurseries.

At Noon we returned on board and found our traders had

[1] The Polynesians, to which racial group the Tahitians belong, are of heterogeneous descent and—as Robertson noted—of wide variety of pigmentation, the ladies of the whitest sort being the most sparing in their favours to the *Dolphin*'s crew. At the time of the visit, the Polynesians occupied an oceanic triangle whose corners were New Zealand, Easter Island and Hawaii, with a common language and many common social and religious customs. Their migrations, in balsa-wood rafts and in their great sailing-canoes, are still the subejct of learned speculations.

[2] *A mustee:* a cross between white and quadroon, was seven-eighths white.

but very indifferent success, they only brought off four pigs, a few fowls and some fruit. I was told by one of the Young Gentlemen that a new sort of trade took up the most of their attention this day, but it might be more properly called the old trade. He says a Dear Irish boy, one of our Marines, was the first that began the trade, for which he got a very severe thrashing from the Liberty men for not beginning in a more decent manner, in some house, or at the back of some bush or tree. Paddy's Excuse was the fear of losing the Honour of having the first.

7 *July* WE had fine Moderate pleasant weather, with regular Sea and Land breezes. After dinner we sent the trading party ashore to endeavour to produce some more Hogs, but they got none, and returned on board with only a few bunches of Plantains and Bananas, but the old trade went on merrily. This night we had fine pleasant weather with refreshing showers, which still brought off a sweet and agreeable smell. From Eight to ten P.M. we saw great numbers of Lights on the SW reef, and some lights along-shore close by the Water-side. I suppose they were all fishing.

At Sunrise we sent the traders, Waterers and Liberty men Ashore, and for fear of their not succeeding better nor yesterday, Mr. Gore was sent with a party of twenty Armed men to trade along-shore from House to house, beginning at the foot of Skirmish hill and to come up to the watering-place. At Noon all hands returned on board but neither party had great success. The old traders brought off but three small pigs, some fowls, and a little fruit, and Mr Gore's party brought off four Small Hogs and two pigs, with some very fine Red and White Yams. He likeways brought off a very fine Shell, and some beautiful Mother-of-pearl fish-hooks and two pearl oyster-shells.

The Gunner and his party still keep the natives at a great distance and never suffer any of them to stay on his side the River, but the Liberty men still carry on a friendly Correspondence with the natives, and neither of them seems to be afraid

73

of the other. We this day served all the Seamen fresh pork and good broth, and all the Warrant and Petty Officers was served two fowls amongst three men and as much fruit as they chose to take. Our first Lieut. now turned very sick, when the Captain began to recover, but most of the Seamen is now pretty well. All those who are able to go Ashore recover fast.

*8 July* WE had fine pleasant weather, with a regular sea and Land breeze. This day the Captain Landed for the first time, and walked a little way along shore, and seemed greatly refreshed on his return on board the Ship. All night we had fine pleasant breezes with some refreshing Showers.

This evening I observed a great fire at or near the Altar—but know not what they were about, but they kept it up from sunset to ten at night. There was no Lights appeared on either reef this night. At Sunrise the Gunner and his party, with the Waterers and Liberty men, all Landed at the old trading place, but Mr Gore's Party was not sent ashore, as he says the whole of the Natives' stock from the N side of Skirmish Hill to the River side, is all Exhausted, therefore it would be idle to search there any more. This forenoon I saw Casey making out the plan of this Bay, and one of the Young Gentlemen who had the charge of the Watch on Deck came down and told me he saw a great Number of very large vessels coming round the SW reef and above three times the number of men on the Reef that he ever saw before.

At this time the Captain and Second Lieut. with the Doctor was all Ashore taking the Air with a party of men under Arms to protect them. I immediately went up to Deck and Viewed them with a very fine Spy-Glass of the Captain's, and saw them coming round the Reef all under Sail. At first they appeared like large Schooners or Sloops, but when they came round the reef I got a much fairer view of them, and Compared them with the Great double Canoe which the Captain and I saw on the reef near the Altar.

They all went round a point of land about a mile and a half

from where this canoe lay, and as near as I could imagine there was about ten or twelve of them near double her burden, and the rest was all smaller. From their first coming in sight I observed them all wearing long streamers like Pendants, of Red, White and Blue, and some looked Yellow. The instant they came round the Reef several small Canoes came out of the place where they went in, to welcome them and returned back with them after waiting about ten minutes. When they all made this stop the whole Shore-side abreast of them was full of people, and all the people on the Reef went Ashore after them. When they stopped, the whole of these large Vessels appeared full of men, and so great a number of people on the Shore, with a great number of small Canoes gathering round them, made me suppose they had some designs of making another Attack upon us: but when I saw them all disappear together I began to think they were Strangers come from some other Country, Or some trading Vessels that had been some distant voyage, and all their friends and acquaintances welcoming them home. The Large Vessels all appeared to be Loaded with something, but the particulars I know not.

When the Captain returned On board I informed him of what I had seen, and proposed going to see what sort of River or harbour they were gone into. He at first approved of my going, or the Second Lieut., but afterwards thought it running too great a risk to let the Boats go out of sight of the Ship. This was Acting with much more prudence nor my curiosity would have allowed me to do at this time, but on a Serious reflection I believe the Satisfying of my curiosity at this time, might have been the loss of some Lives to the Natives of this Island, and perhaps some of our own. But when I think of the affair of the Jolly-boat, when I first found out this Bay, after that I think there would be no great risk of our Barge and Cutter Examining any of their fleets with twenty-Six well Armed men, which the two boats could carry with great Ease, indeed I must own it is very possible.

We might have been attacked and put under the disagreeable necessity of firing amongst the Seamen belonging to this Fleet, and perhaps we might have killed some of them, but I can hardly think we ran any risk of our Boats or Lives, and if they did not attack us we would never have hurt any of them. After this we saw several large Vessels come round this point, and go into the same River or harbour, but we never took the least notice of them. At noon the traders and Liberty men returned on board and brought off three pigs, a dozen fowls and some fruit. This day all hands was served fresh pork and plenty of Good broth.

*9 July* WE had Moderate fine pleasant weather, with regular Sea and Land Breezes. After dinner the trading party and Liberty men went Ashore and brought off four pigs and Eight Fowls. Our Liberty men and the Natives is now turned so friendly that they walk Arm-in-Arm. About sunset the Captain went to take the Air in his Barge, but returned very poorly. At Night we had a fine Brisk breeze with some refreshing showers. None of the Natives appeared on the Reef this night.

At Sunrise we sent ashore the traders, Waterers and Liberty men, and Mr Gore with a party of men to cut fire-wood, at the N end of Skirmish Hill. When the Wooders began to cut down the first Tree, a great Number of the natives Assembled, and began to be very uneasy, and one old man made a long talk, and seemed very unhappy, and I suppose thought we intended to cut all the trees down. But when Mr Gore found this old man was the owner, he made him understand that we only wanted but ten or twelve trees, and gave the Owner a Seven-inch Spike-Nail for the tree that he cut down, and drove in Another Nail in the Next old tree, and pointed to the old man to take it out, and made the men cut it down directly. This pleased the Owner so well that he soon pointed out more trees than we had occasion for. None of them had ever seen a Spike-Nail before this. The old man took a delight in showing his Nails to his friends and seemed highly pleased with the bargain.

76

At Noon all hands returned On board and brought off two Hogs and two pigs and some fruit. This day the Gunner purchased some very beautiful Shells, for a Sixpenny Nail and some Pearls for buttons and some Mother-of-Pearl fish-hooks for ten-penny Nails. We this day got up the Forge and set the Armourer and his Mate to make some small Iron Gouges, thinking the Natives would like that much better nor Nails. But in this we was mistaken for they preferred nails before any one thing we had.

I this day went Ashore for the first time, and Walked about a mile up the River, with two of the Young Gentlemen along with me, and one of the Seamen with a Musket.

The two Young men had a Cutlass each, and I carried a pistol and a broad-sword. We walked past several regular well-built Houses, but saw very little live-stock about them, and Scarce any kind of furniture in these Houses. I suppose fear has made them remove everything of Value back in to the country. I saw only two kinds of trees growing on this River side, which was the Bread-fruit and what we called the Apple-tree; it seems they permit no barren trees to cumber the low grounds here. We passed several of the Natives going down with fruit to the market-place. They all stopped and stared awhile at us, but none of them Attempted to turn us back or Molest us in the least.

In place of being offended at our going a little back in their country, in my Opinion and the Young Gentlemen's they rather seemed pleased. I saw no underwood here of any kind; they seem to take a great deal of pains to keep the Roots of the trees clean. Here I saw some nurseries of young trees Walled in with Stones about three foot high.

In returning back to the boats, three very fine Young Girls accosted us, and one of them made a Signal and smiled in my face. This made me stop to enquire what the Young Lady wanted, and supposing the Young Gentlemen better acquainted nor me, who had never seen any of the Young Ladies before, but at a great distance, I desired one of them to Explain the meaning of the Signal. They both put on a very

77

Grave look and told me they did not understand her Signs. I then supposed she had something to sell, made signs for her to show her goods, but this seemed to displease her and Another repeated the same Signal, which was this, she held up her right hand and first finger of the right hand straight, then laid hold of her right wrist with the left hand, and held the Right hand and first finger up straight and smiled, then crooked all her fingers and kept playing with them and Laughed very hearty, which set my young friends a Laughing as hearty as the Young Girl. This made me insist upon their Explaining the Sign, and they told me the Young Girls only wanted a Long Nail each, but they never before saw them make a sign for one longer nor their fingers, but they supposed the Young Girls thought I carried longer nails nor the rest because I was dressed in a different manner. I wanted them to explain the other part of the signal, that I might understand the whole, but the young men begged to be excused. I therefore gave the Young Girls a nail each, and parted good friends, then walked down to see how the traders went on, and told the Gunner what had happened betwixt us and the Young Girls, and he Explained the whole matter in few words, and told me my young friends was not so very Ignorant as they pretended to be. He likewise told me that the price of the old trade, is now fixed at a thirty-penny nail each time, and he told me that the Liberty men dealt so largely in that way—that he was much afraid of losing his trade of Hogs, Pigs, fowls and fruit.

He said the people of this Country deal very cunningly. If they bring down three or four different things to sell, they always endeavour to sell the worst first, and if they get what they want for any trifling thing that they can easily Spare they carry back their Hogs, pigs and fowls. He likewise says he has often seen them conceal their best things, until he purchased the other things of less value. This made him afraid that the natives would purchase all the nails and toys by means of the old trade, and of Course bring no other Goods to market, therefore Advised me to endeavour to put a stop to it, when I went on board, by preventing the Liberty men from coming ashore.

This I told him was out of my power, as the most of them was on the Sick list. He then told me the Sickest of them traded a little, therefore could not be so very bad as they pretended on board. I then promised to represent the case to the commanding officer on board and the Surgeon. He then said my young friends dealt a little, which might likewise be prevented, if I represented it properly on board, but they excused themselves by affirming that he dealt more largely nor any of them, therefore was the greatest spoiler of the trade himself. I then saw how trade went on and advised them to agree, and all deal moderately for fear of losing the fresh broth and other Good things.

When I returned on board I acquainted the Second Lieut. who was then Commanding Officer, the Captain and first Lieut. then being Sick. I then let him and the Doctor, and our good Merry friend the purser know how trade went on shore. We then Consulted what was best to be done. Some was of Opinion it would be best to detain the Liberty men some day, others said it would be ruining all trade to keep them on board, and the Doctor, who was certainly a man that took the greatest care of his patients, Affirmed that the keeping the Liberty men confined on board the Ship would ruin their health and Constitution for, said he, anything that depresses the mind and spirits of men must certainly hurt them.

We sent for a few which was in the sick list, and Examined them, and threatened to stop their liberty for spoiling the Gunner's trade. This affected the poor unthinking fellows so much, that we immediately saw a visible change in their Countenance, which plainly confirmed what the Doctor said was very Just. We therefore agreed to prevent them as much as possible from taking Nails and toys Ashore with them. We likewise put a very necessary Question to the Doctor, who Affirmed upon his Honour that no man on board was affected with any sort of disorder, that they could communicate to the Natives of this beautiful Island.

*10 July*  W E had moderate fine pleasant weather with a regular sea and Land breeze. After dinner the traders and wooders was both sent ashore and at sunset they both returned on board. The traders brought off a few fowls and some fruit, and the wooders brought off two boat-Loads of fire-wood. The Natives pointed out the Oldest trees for us to cut down, and Mr Gore took great care that none of his party should hurt any tree, but what they pointed out. This pleased the natives greatly, and several of them Assisted to carry down the cut wood, which made Gore give them a sixpenny nail each. This they thought so high Wages, that they ever after carried all the Wood down. The most difficulty that Mr Gore had after this, was to keep his men from straggling into the Woods, for now they had lost all thoughts of fear, as the Natives and them was now quite intimate, therefore both he and the Gunner agreed to let them have a stroll through the Woods in turn. This plan made all parties pleased. At Night we had a great many Squally Showers but not much wind in them.

At sunrise we sent the traders Ashore to the usual place, and the Wooders to the Northward of the River, as there appeared to be several old trees there. They purchased the trees here for a large Spike-Nail the same as the other place. The method was this, our people stuck in the nail to the tree and desired the Owner to take it out. If he took out the nail and kept it, they cut down the Tree, but if they returned the Nail or pointed to another tree then the first tree was let stand and the other cut down.

One of the Young Gentlemen told me that there was a great dispute happened this day between two of the Natives where he stuck in the Nail to pay for the tree. An old man took it out who, it seems, was the Owner of the tree and had his House Close by it, but another stout well-looking man who seemed to be one of their chiefs took the nail from the old man and kept it. He says there was a good many ill-natured words passed betwixt them, and the old man gave up the point, and went in to his house.

A few minutes after there came down a fine well-looking woman of the dark Mustee colour, with a great many men along with her, who seemed to pay her a great deal of respect. Some of these was standing by when the dispute happened betwixt the two men, and told her what had happened and she spoke to one that stood by her, who called to the old man, who immediately appeared before her trembling. She spoke to him a few words, but the old man scarce made any Answer. She then talked to him that had the nail, and he immediately gave up the nail to the old man, and walked off seemingly in great fear, and this Woman spoke to him very Angry-like, and soon after walked into the woods with the man who came down with her. This in my Opinion plainly demonstrates, that there is both Justice, and Property in this happy Island.

At Noon all the traders, Wooders and Liberty men came off to Dinner and brought off two of the natives to Dine with them. The one was the old man's Son who assisted the Gunner, but the other was one of their chiefs or great men. He appeared to be a Sensible well-behaved man, about thirty years of Age, and about five foot nine, well made and very good features of a dark Mustee colour.

We showed him the Ship, and he took very particular notice of everything which we showed him, and seemed greatly surprised at the construction of our ship. This day the Captain and first Lieut. was both able to sit up, and we all Dined in the Gun-room, with the chief along with us.

After spreading the cloth we all sat down and made him sit down in a chair, but before he sat down he viewed the chair all round, then sat down and viewed the plates, knives and forks with great attention, but the instant he saw the Dinner set down, he laid down his plate and touched nothing until he was helped.

We had a very Excellent dinner, which consisted of Broth made with two fine fat fowls, two ditto roasted, a roasted pig, roasted yams, Plantains, Bananas, Soft Bread, biscuit apple-pudding and apple-pie. All of this he eat a part of, and took very great notice of the manner that we eat with our Spoons, knives and forks, and used them in the same manner that we did and helped himself with fowl, pig, yams etc. the same as we did.

We had very Good claret, Madeira, port, Rum and Brandy Grog and excellent good London porter, but his choice was water. He smelt and tasted the Wine and Grog but liked neither but hob-nobbed with water and seemed greatly pleased when we all touched Glasses with him. He observed us wipe our mouths before we drank, with our pocket-handkerchiefs. This made him a little uneasy, he having nothing of that kind, and seemed unwilling to use his clothes; I therefore gave him the corner of the table-cloth to wipe his mouth, which so shocked the delicate Mr Clarke that he could neither eat nor drink any more at that time, but kept growling at the chief and me for being so very indelicate, all the time we sit at dinner. He took up the cloth several times, and Endeavoured to make the man understand how unpolite it was to use the cloth. This made the man unhappy for some time, as he could not comprehend his meaning. He still thought he had done something very bad, which began to make me uneasy, knowing myself to be the Original author of this man's trouble.

I therefore, in order to please the Chief, hob-nobbed with him and used the corner of the Cloth, and made him do the same, and began to be very merry with him, which pleased the man so much that he made Signs to poor Growl, who was still on the fret, that he would bring him a fine young Girl to sleep with him. This Merry thought of the Chief put an end to growling, and pleased the fretter, who was pleased to say well done Jonathan if you perform your promise you shall be rewarded, this being the first Christian name that was ever bestowed on any of the natives of this Island. We always after called this man Jonathan.

After Dinner we showed Jonathan a looking-Glass which surprised him a little at first, but he soon began to pull his Beard, which is the custom of his country. Then he got a pair of tweezers which he applied to the proper use, and began to pull his beard and the hairs out of his nose, but the thing which pleased and Astonished Jonathan most of all, was the picture of a very handsome well-dressed young Lady, in Miniature, which the Doctor Showed him.

We made him understand that this was a picture of the women in our country, and if he went with us he should have one of them always to Sleep with. This put him in such raptures of Joy that it is impossible for me to describe. He hugged the picture in his breast, and kissed it twenty times, and made several other odd motions, to show us how happy he would be with so fine a woman. We all supposed Jonathan to be one of the first-rank people of the Island, from the respect that the rest showed him, but had he been King of this and all the high Mountains to the Southward, let them reach or Extend ever so far, even to the Dutch Spice Islands, I am certain Jonathan would have made this Young Lady Queen, had the Substance been here in place of the Shadow—nay more, I really believe he would have come to England for her had we been willing to take him with us, and his friends contented to let him go.

[Ibbott records that the Armourer's Forge was again at work this day and the next. A seaman called Horsnail saw it busy once more on 21 July.]

*11 July* WE had a fresh Gale with Cloudy weather and some Squally Showers, the Wind at ESE all the twenty-four hours. After dinner, our traders and Wooders went Ashore with the Liberty men, and at sunset the Captain and first Lieut. went ashore to take the air, but both returned back very poorly. When they landed our friend Jonathan at the North point of the Bay he was immediately received by a great number of his Countrymen, who all seemed very happy at the Accounts which he gave them of his reception on board the Ship. The Captain made Jonathan several presents, and some of his friends, and all parted Good Friends. At Sunset all the traders,

83

Wooders and Liberty men returned on board, and brought off two boat-loads of Wood, but no Hogs, fowls nor fruit. Scarce any of the Natives came down to the trading place; the whole waited at the North point of the Bay to receive our friend Jonathan. At Night we had a fresh Gale with several Squally Showers. None of the natives appeared on the reef this night, neither saw we any fires on the shore.

At Sunrise we sent all the traders, wooders and Liberty men ashore. Our trading party had very bad success this day, they only brought us off two fowls and some fruit. What was the reason of this bad day's trade I know not, but it was the worst we ever had. I was told some time after that this bad day's trade was owing to some dispute amongst our own people, about a thing which they had too great plenty of and at a very low price. At Noon all hands came on board to Dinner, and our friend Jonathan came off in a Canoe with four men paddling him, and two very handsome Young Girls, which he brought off to Dine with us. We immediately got in Jonathan and the two Mustee Girls, and carried them all through the Ship, and showed them everything that was curious, supposing them to be his two Sisters; but when he came down to the Gun-room, he made us understand that he brought them off Agreeable to his promise, in order to make up matters with Mr Clarke he offered him the choice of either.[1]

*12 July*  WE had moderate fine pleasant weather with the Wind at ESE. After dinner we sent the Wooders, traders and Liberty men ashore. The Wooders brought off two boat-Loads of Wood and paid for the two as usual, and the traders got three pigs, some fowls and a good Deal of fruit, and purchased several curiosities from the natives, such as pearls, Pearl oyster-shells, Mother-of-pearl fish-hooks, and some lines made of Silk Grass as neat as any fishing-lines in England, and made after the same manner. At night we had fine pleasant weather

[1] Nothing in Lieut. Clarke's Journal indicates his choice, and it is probable that he spurned both.

with some refreshing showers; we saw both Reefs full of people with Lights.

At Sunrise we sent the traders, Wooders and Liberty men ashore. I this day landed for the second time, and Walked from the River side to the foot of Skirmish Hill, where I saw several Houses all regularly built, and Straight Sticks set up on end and large pillars in each corner and one, two or three in the middle, which support a very neat well-thatched Roof. Several of them had little division in their houses, but I saw no kind of furniture but cocoa shells for drinking out of, and some Calabashes for the same use, a few Wooden trays made after the same manner that our Butcher's trays is, and plenty of Mats of Various sizes which I suppose serves them for Bedding. I saw no trees here but the Bread-fruit, apple and plantain trees, which was all kept very clean about the Roots. Where these trees grows it is a very fat Black soil capable of producing any kind of tropical fruit, that's to be found in the West Indies.

Here I saw several Images of Men and Women set up close by their Houses, rudely carved out of a large tree. On one of those trees there was five human figures cut out, and all standing the one on the top of the other's head. The lowermost was a man; on the top of his head there stood a Woman fully as large as the man; on the top of her head there stood another man, but much smaller nor the man below; on his head there stood another Woman about his own size, and on the top of all there was a great stout fellow with all his parts proportionable. The others had some two, others three and some four Images cut out, but the uppermost was always the largest, and a man. They are none of the finest carvers, but they take care to imitate nature so Exact, that no man can mistake the sex which they mean to represent.

I kept viewing these Images some time, until a few of the natives came round me; I then began to handle them and look very gravely to see how they would behave, but they only smiled and said nothing. I then laid hold of one of them and led him up to the Image, but could not prevail with him to touch it. I then pushed at it with my broad-sword to see how

85

they would behave then, but still they kept smiling one to the other. I then cut a little bit off one of the men with the Sword, then they turned round and walked off but did not seem anyways Angry. This behaviour makes one suppose they do not set up those Images to Worship them. I rather suppose they are set up to Commemorate some of their families after death.[1]

As I walked up to the Watering-place, I met some of the Natives with pieces of Sugar-cane in their hand, and purchased a piece for a small nail, but found it was not near so sweet as the Canes which is cultivated in the West Indian Islands. When I got up to the trading place I found the Gunner had got a very fine roasted pig from the old man that Assists him in the trading way. I eat a part of it with the Gunner and the old man and some of the Young Gentlemen; it was as well dressed and Clean as any pig I ever saw. Leadenhall Market could not have produced a finer pig nor this was; the old man brought it from his own house wrapped up in Green Leaves of the Plantain tree. At Noon we all went on board and carried off a Hog, two pigs, some fowls and plenty of fruit.

*13 July*  THE weather was variable—the first part of the Day we had fine clear weather with the wind at E and SE. After Dinner we sent the Wooders, traders and Liberty men ashore, and our old friend Jonathan came off to pay us another visit and brought off two fine roasted pigs with him and some fruit. We Enquired after the two young Girls, and he made signs that they were crying Ashore but could not get off from their friends; but if the two Gentlemen who was most friendly to them would go ashore and sleep with them there, the young Girls would be very happy—but the young Girls' lovers would not trust themselves Ashore all night for fear of Accidents.

At Sunset all our people returned On board and the traders brought off three Hogs, three pigs, some fowls and plenty of fruit, and the Wooders brought off a boat-load of Wood. At

[1] Images were regarded either as representations of gods, intermittently inhabited by them, or as vehicles of prayer to them.

the same time Jonathan's canoe came off for him and he went Ashore, but seemed greatly disappointed that none of us would go Ashore with him. We had a great deal of Rain all this Night.

At Sunrise we saw a great many of the natives at work, cutting through the Beach to let the river run into the sea right abreast of the Ship. I suppose their intention for doing this was to prevent the river from over-flowing their Low grounds. The Beach was all sand and much higher nor the low grounds. It rained very hard the remaining part of this Day, which prevented us from sending any of our Boats ashore, but our friend Jonathan and the old man came off and brought a roasted pig each. The old man paid a great deal of respect to Jonathan and was always ready to do whatever he seemed to desire him.

Mr Furneaux and I rigged out Jonathan with a complete Suit of Clothes, shoes etc. We had plenty of diversion showing him how to put all the Clothes on, especially the Breeches. They puzzled him worst of all, but after he found out how to use them he seemed more fond of them than all the rest, except the shoes. They pleased him greatly and he walked up and down the Deck with great spirits. After dinner he went ashore in his English dress and seemed Extremely happy when our Boat Landed him. He called to some of the country people to carry him out for fear of wetting his shoes, and when he came to the river he made two of his servants carry him over, but before he always waded through the River without any kind of ceremony.

When he got across the River a great many of his Country people came round him and he took great pleasure of showing himself—but what became of this Jolly young fellow afterwards we know not, as we never saw nor heard anything more of him. We supposed the young man's friends was afraid of his going off with us, and had ordered him back into the country to prevent him.

I am almost certain that this same Jonathan would have come with us much sooner nor stayed behind. Had this man come with us, I dare say he would have soon learned the

English Language, and being a sensible fine smart man, he certainly would have been able to give us a much fuller account both of his own and the Adjacent Countries than it was possible for us to learn, without walking through all the country and being at the Greatest pain to discover everything that was curious—which was out of our power to do as we was circumstanced.[1]

[Captain Wallis states that the Queen came aboard the *Dolphin* this day, and that he gave her 'a large Blue Mantle that reached from her Head to her Heels'. He 'tied it with Ribbons, and gave her several sorts of Beads, and a Looking-Glass and many other things'.]

*14 July*   WE had Moderate Gales and Cloudy weather with a great deal of Rain, and the wind from ESE to SE. The first part of the day we sent no boats ashore, nor saw we any of the natives moving out of their houses. It Rained very hard all night but cleared up a little in the morning. We then sent all our boats to trade and bring off wood and water, but let no Liberty men go ashore. In a very little time after our men Landed it began to Rain very hard, which made the Country people all go home to their houses and obliged our people to come off; but the Gunner brought off four Hogs and two dozen of fowls. We now served fresh pork every day; it makes exceedingly good broth for all hands.

The Gunner told me an old woman came down to the River side this day and cried a long time, then made a young man that stood by her, bring over a large bough of a plantain tree. When he came over he made a very long speech then laid down his bough and brought over the old woman, and made another man bring over two fine Large hogs. When the old woman came over she looked very hard at all our people and began to Cry again, and he says the tears run down the old

[1] Jonathan, with his English suit, appeared two years later to welcome the *Endeavour*, when he recognized Gore and was recognized by him.

Woman's cheeks at a great rate, which shocked him very much, not knowing what could be the meaning of all the poor Woman's sorrow. After the man had done with his second speech, the old woman begun to Explain the whole matter, and made him Understand that we had killed her Husband and three sons. Then the poor old Woman fell a crying again, and was not able to stand until she was supported by two young men that Appeared to be her sons or some very near relations, that took a great deal of care of her. When she recovered herself again she Ordered one of the Young Men to deliver the two Hogs to the Gunner, and shook hands with him but would receive nothing for them, altho' he offered the old Woman ten times as much as he paid in common for Hogs of the same size. This poor old woman was clothed with Red Cloth,[1] which is the mourning that they wear in this Country. This he says the old man Explained to him, and Afterwards showed him a good many more that was in Mourning for their friends which was killed at the time when they attacked.

All the rest of the people, both men and women, are clothed with a sort of White Cloth which they make out of the inner rind of a sort of Willow.

*15 July* WE had fine pleasant weather with a few showers of Rain, and a regular sea and land breeze. The first part of the day we sent no boats from the Ship. At Sunset we saw a great smoke at the altar, and the fire Continued till ten at night, but what they were about I know not. There was a great number of lights on the Reefs from seven to ten at night, and several lights all along shore. There was more of them Employed fishing this night, nor any other two nights that we had lain here.

At sunrise we sent all our boats for Wood and water and a

---

[1] Red was, in fact, not a mourning but a ceremonial colour: and the cloth was *tapa*, which, unwoven, is made in Polynesia generally from the bark of the Paper Mulberry (*Broussonetia Papyrifera*). The bark is beaten out with a wooden mallet.

party to trade as usual. After Breakfast we let twenty men go ashore as usual on Liberty. This day trade went on tolerably well. The Gunner brought off four Hogs and four pigs, ten fowls and plenty of fruit and some yams, he likewise purchased several very fine Shells, Mother-of-Pearl fish-hooks, and a few Pearls and several other curious things.

[Despite Robertson's assertion of trade going 'tolerably well' this day, Captain Wallis records: 'The Gunner complains that the Trade is greatly spoiled by the large Spikes that are stolen from the ship and brought on shore, which the People give the Women so that they will now part with nothing but for twice as much as they did yesterday. Gave orders that every man that goes on shore should be searched before he landed and not to suffer the Women to cross the river.']

*16 July*  W E had Moderate fine pleasant Weather with the Wind at East. The first part of the day we sent no boats Ashore—Except the Barge which the Captain and first Lieut. went to get the Air in. At the North side of the Bay there is a very Long House with several small ones round it, that the Inhabitants have forsaken ever since we arrived here. This long House was built more like a Shade nor one of our Houses, therefore the more open and Airy and the more suitable to this climate. The Captain and first Lieut. Generally walked up and down this House, not being able to bear the heat of the Sun, until he was near set. While they kept under the shade with a guard to attend them, the other Gentlemen who went along with them sometimes Walked a little way into the Woods where there was several little Houses, but never attempted to go any Great distance.

By this time the natives and all our people was turned very sociable, and the Instant our Boats Landed numbers of them came flocking round, especially the young Girls, who very seldom failed to carry off a nail from every man of the party.

I was told by a Gentleman of the party that he had seen a

very handsome little woman, who lived near to this long House, and he says he made her several little presents at different times that he saw her ashore, but could never find her so kind as the other young Girls. This Day he gave her some very considerable presents, at least they appeared so to her, and she gave him the usual Signal, which he readily obeyed, and walked after her into the Woods. When she got clear out of sight of the rest, she pointed to a little House, and made him understand that he should be happily rewarded for all his presents there, but

Just as my friend was going in, he observed a strong well-made man coming towards the House. This made him stop and the Woman observed him waiting at the Door, ran out and saw it was her husband. She immediately looked frightened and called out *takena takena*[1] which made my friend suppose it was her husband. She soon returned to the Door with a very fine fowl and some fruit, and when the Husband came, she was selling the fowl, and my friend was offering double the price that any other fowl cost, but she could not agree until her

[1] *takena:* meaning 'brother', 'cousin' or near relation. It is likely that the man in question was not in fact the woman's husband, but a near relation.

husband came. Then she talked to him and he began to smell, and offered the fowl and fruit for what was offered to his wife, and my friend gladly accepted, and seeing the Husband was a carpenter he gave him several Nails, which gained the poor man's heart so much, that he would have given him all that he had except his handsome wife.

My friend returned to his party very unhappy at so great a disappointment, but I told him I thought he had double reason to be happy, that the strong fellow did not catch him and give him a good drubbing. He allows he was well able, if he had got hold of him without his sword. He told me the Guard relieve one another regularly and get Value for their nail, and return back to their duty. Some of the fellows was so Extravagant that while he was Ashore, they spent two Nails. He says this was owing to the Great Variety of Goods which came to Market.

At Sun-Set our Barge returned on board, and brought off two Pigs, Eight fowls and several bundles of very fine Plantains and Bananas, which was paid with Nails and toys as usual. At Night we had fine pleasant weather with some refreshing Showers. Saw several of the natives fishing along-shore but few up on the Reefs.

At Sunrise the Barge, Cutter and Launch was Manned and Armed, and Mr Furneaux and six of the Young Gentlemen to assist him took the command of the party, and went to the SW side of the Bay to trade for Stock. They Landed between the point of Land where we saw the Great fleet, and the altar which the Captain and I observed, but took no kind of Notice of Either. At 8 A.M. he Landed with thirty Armed men and ordered all the Boats to keep rowing up abreast of the party, that they might always be ready to embark if necessity required it, likeways to take in the Hogs, pigs etc. as he purchased them from the Natives. He said the instant that he landed Great Numbers of the Natives Assembled round them, but all of them came without any kind of Offensive or defensive weapons, and the whole behaved very peaceably and traded very fair and honestly. He immediately Marched toward the Watering-

92

place and bought as many Hogs, fowls etc. as he could get, but says he saw no difference of the country down there, from the coast about the River side—only a few places which was walled in with Stones and Earth that he supposed to be burying Grounds, but took no more notice of them.

At the South Side of Skirmish Hill an old woman made up to him Dressed in Mourning, and made Signs that she had two Sons killed by our Bones—this was the name they gave our great Guns. The poor Woman shed some tears, then gave him a present of a Large hog, and seemed unwilling to receive any reward for the Hog, but he obliged some of her friends that stood by, to take triple value for her Hog. This he says seemed to please them much. After that he Marched over the top of Skirmish Hill, where there was only one large tree growing, where the natives assembled at the last Skirmish we had. He saw the place where the shot fell, which we fired to frighten the natives, and says it was within about twenty yards of the tree. At noon the party returned On board and brought off Seven Hogs, three dozen of fowls, some very fine yams and a Great Quantity of fruit of all sorts that we have yet seen in this Country.

[Captain Wallis records some striking details of his visit this day to the Queen. She carried the ailing officers (himself included) in her own arms. When, much later, Horace Walpole read of this incident in Hawkesworth's *Voyages*, he noted drily: 'Dr. Hawkesworth is provoking. An old black gentlewoman of forty carries Captain Wallis across a river when he was too weak to walk, and the man represents them as a new edition of Dido and Aeneas.'

The Queen made her people kiss Wallis's hand.

'She made us all sit down,' he says, 'then she called four young girls who took down my stockings and shoes and pulled off my coat, and they smoothed down the skin, gently chafing it. She likewise had the same operation performed on the first Lieutenant and Purser . . . After a certain time, I believe near half an hour, they left off and dressed me again, at which they were very awkward, however I found that it had done me much service and the others declared the same.'

What startled every Tahitian was the doctor's act in removing his wig. 'Every eye was fixed on the prodigy,' said Wallis, 'and every operation was suspended.'

The Queen apparently tied round each of the principal officers' necks 'wreaths of hair knotted together and worked like sennet [1] and she made signs it was her own hair and work'.]

*17 July* WE had fine pleasant weather, with the Wind Easterly. The first part of the day we sent no boats ashore to trade, but the Captain went to take the Air at the long house on the North side of the Bay, where numbers of the natives assembled as usual, and trade went on the same as yesterday. Every man laid out his nail, and some two.

The Handsome little woman brought my friend a fine large pig, and her Husband brought a large bundle of fruit, and wanted to make him a present of all, but he obliged them to take triple value, and made signs for them to come on board the Ship, but the man seemed unwilling to come on board, but the little woman pointed to the Ship and called out *Mettaccow Mettaccow Mettaccow*,[2] which in their Language Signifies tomorrow.

At sunset the Barge returned On board and brought off two pigs, six fowls and some fruit. At Night we had fine pleasant weather but no rain. From seven to nine both reefs was full of Lights and several along the Shore.

At Sunrise we sent the Gunner and his party to trade at the old place, and gave liberty to twenty men to go and ramble up and down, in sight of the Guard that Attended the Gunner, but not to attempt to go into the Woods under no less penalty nor being flogged severely. These orders was given to prevent any accidents, as our men had now laid aside all manner of fear.

[1] Sennet is flat, braided cordage.

[2] Probably, as Robertson suggests, tomorrow: *mata ao*, literally 'the beginning of the day'.

Two or three would frequently venture a mile into the wood, and hold a sort of conference with forty or fifty of the natives, and sometimes one would go in far as any of the Young Girls chose to Carry him, and perhaps pass by a hundred of the Natives, and none of them attempt to molest him; this friendly behaviour of the Natives made some on board suppose they had a treacherous design, therefore it was always thought proper to Endeavour to keep every man on his Guard.

A little after nine A.M. the handsome little woman came off in a canoe, with her Husband, Father and Mother and a Young Girl which we supposed to be her Sister. We showed them all the Different parts of the Ship, and the Husband took very great notice of everything he saw, Especially the chairs, chests and Tables. He observed every Joint in the Chairs and Tables, and measured the length and breadth of every Joint of our Chairs and the Gun-room table, and marked his measures on a piece of Line, which he brought with him. I observed him make different knots for the Length and breadth. He appears to be a very Sensible fellow and I dare say will be able to make a Chair or Table when he has a mind.

While the honest Carpenter and I was taking the dimensions of the Chairs and tables, my friend and the Wife was endeavouring to get clear of the Old Man and his wife, and Another hand took care of the Sister and Showed her some curious things which pleased the young lass: but the instant the Carpenter saw his wife and my friend go into his Cabin, he immediately went after them to see what curiosities they had there. This disappointment cost my friend a suit of old Clothes to the honest Carpenter, and a shirt to the Wife, besides the trouble of showing the curious man everything in his Cabin.

At this time the Woman slipped out of the Cabin, and cast loose the Canoe which she came off in, and let her run a good way from the Ship. The wind being ahead soon carried her near sixty yards from the ship. She then looked round and saw her father and Mother was out of the Gun-room, and one of the Young Gentlemen entertaining her sister. She then called out loudly to her husband and told him the canoe was gone adrift. This made the poor man throw off his clothes, to jump into the water to save his Canoe. This alarmed my friend, who desired me to be so good as order a boat to go After the canoe. Mean-time he laid hold of the Carpenter to prevent him from jumping overboard, but the little artful creature immediately put herself in such a passion that her husband twisted himself out of my friend's hands and jumped out at the Gun-room port and swum after his canoe.

The instant that he was in the water, she immediately stepped into my friend's cabin and laid hold of his coat and pulled him in. While she was Enjoying the reward of her Art and Cunning, the poor man's Life was running the Greatest risk imaginable, not knowing but he might be Devoured every minute by some large Shark such as we caught about a fort-night before: but the honest Carpenter had better luck; in about ten minutes' time he brought his canoe back and made her fast to the Gun-room port where his wife cast her loose from, and jumped into the Gun-room where his Wife received him, and gave him a few large nails which she gained in his Absence, to make up for the loss he sustained. This Greatly pleased the good man, as he knowed nothing of the way and manner the nails was procured.

Then they all got a few presents and was sent Ashore in one of our boats which towed their canoe.

At noon all our traders and Liberty men returned On board and brought off Six pigs, Eight fowls, some Yams and a great quantity of Plantains, Bananas and Apples—but no Bread-fruit.

*18 July* WE had Moderate fine pleasant weather with the wind at ESE. After dinner sent the traders, Waterers and liberty men Ashore. This day our Liberty men cut great quantities of very fine Grass along the River-side, and brought it down to the Liberty tent, where they Afterwards made it into Hay which Served all our Sheep to Tinian. At Sunset all hands returned on board, and brought off Six small Hogs, some fowls and plenty of fruit.

The Gunner now told me, that there was a great alteration of the prices at Market, what he now buys is a hundred per cent dearer nor the first week that we Landed; this he says is chiefly owing to the Liberty men, who gives too high a price for all sorts of curiosities that they deal in. At night we had fine pleasant weather but saw none of the natives fishing on the Reefs nor yet along Shore. At sunrise we sent the traders, wooders, Waterers and Liberty men Ashore.

I this day went ashore for the third time and took one of the Young Gentlemen, and one of the Seamen along with me. We was all well Armed, and I purposed to go to the top of one of the Hills in order to get a better view of the country nor it was possible to get in the Low Lands, but in this I was greatly disappointed, for the instant we got half way up the Hill we observed the Ship make the Signal for all boats to come on board. As I could not know the Reason for this Signal being made, we returned back without being able to observe any one thing Except two young Girls Washing of Cloths [1] in a little run of Water.

The way they went to work was this: they had a fine smooth broad stone which they laid the cloth on, then they beat it with two pieces of iron-wood the same as they do in Bleach-fields at home. On the Side of the Hill the soil is all of a reddish cast. But being afraid of Losing our passage off in the boats we was not able to Examine it narrowly.

By the time we got down to the Landing place, all the people was in the boats and the Gunner told me he had waited me some time, and was afraid of being reprimanded by Mr Clarke, who ordered the Signal to be made, and soon after sent the Jolly-boat to order all hands On board. And if anyone had strolled away in the Woods, he ordered the Gunner to let them wait for another opportunity, even if it was me, as he knew no business that I had going out of the way more nor he did when he went Ashore. I then told the Gunner that

[1] They were probably making *tapa* cloth.

if he had done amiss in waiting for me, I should bear the Blame.

The Gunner carried off Eight small Hogs, some fowls, and some fruit, and we got On board an hour before the usual time. I Enquired what was the reason of the boats being Ordered On board so soon, but the Young Gentlemen who had the Watch could not inform me, but they told the Gunner to wait on Mr Clarke directly. What passed between them I know not.

I sent in word to the Captain that I was come on board and went down to my Cabin, where I heard no more of this affair till dinner. Then Mr Clarke told me he was surprised how I had detained the boats from coming off after the Signal was made. I told him I was a good way back in the Country when I observed it, and made all the haste to get down that was possible. He then gave a Sneer, and told me he Supposed I was disappointed in finding out Gold and Silver mines. I told him that it was very possible, and I knew no Reason for there not being such things in this Country, as well as in South America under the same parallel, and by all Accounts the Country here has the same appearance as Chile and Brazil. He then said I might have stayed and looked for Gold and Silver mines but not kept the boats. I acknowledged the boats ought to have come off on seeing the Signal, but as there was no kind of necessity for them on board but to disappoint me from finding Gold and Silver Mines, that end was best Answered by letting me come on board. For had I been left with the Young Gentleman and the Quarter-master who was along with me, we would have gone as far in Search of such trifling things, as the Light of the Day would have permitted us to go and return.

There was a good many more words passed between Mr Clarke and me, which obliged me to say, if the only intention of our Voyage was to procure good Eating, we had no Occasion to go farther than our market-place: but I supposed it was our duty, to find out what was the produce of the Country, as well as to find out Good refreshments, as that might some time be of service to the trade of our Country.

His Answer to this was, damn trade. I then begged he would drop the subject for the present, which was done—and the poor growling man retired to his cabin very bad.

At this time the Captain was very bad and the Second Lieut. began to complain, who was a Gentle Agreeable well behaved Good man, and very humane to all the Ship's company. This disheartened most of the Ship's company very much seeing both the Captain and Second Lieut. very bad, and the First beginning to recover, who was heartily hated by all On board. This unhappy tempered man seemingly took a delight in crossing every Officer on board except the Gunner, who was his favourite.

*19 July* WE had Moderate fine pleasant weather with a regular Sea and Land Wind. The first part of the day old Growl would not permit any Boat to go Ashore to trade. At Night we had fine pleasant weather with some refreshing Showers. Saw great Numbers of Lights on the SW Reef and several fishing along shore.

At Sunrise all the traders and Liberty men was ordered Ashore, and trade went much brisker nor ever it did before, which made the Gunner send off word, that he and his party, which consisted of four young Gentlemen, a Sergeant and Sixteen men was all to dine Ashore, if agreeable to the Captain. This I acquainted the Captain of, and he gave his consent, and ordered me to send for the Liberty men, and bring off as many of them as chose to come to Dinner. This I did, but the most of them was glad of the Opportunity of Staying, and none but four came off.

While the rest was at Dinner Mr Pickersgill and the Serjeant Strolled a great way into the Woods, where they fell in with a great number of the natives Assembled together at a very long House where there was a very great entertainment preparing for all the Assembly, at which the Queen of the Country was present, and dressed in mourning. At first they were both Afraid, and would have willingly come off without going too

99

near the Assembly, but several of the natives came towards them, and Invited them to the feast. They were both afraid to disoblige them, knowing that they were a great way from the Guard, and scarce knew their way Back, therefore accepted the Invitation and sat down along with the Natives, until Dinner was ready.

Mr Pickersgill told me the Dinner was dressed at some distance, where there was several little Houses. When it was ready they all formed a Ring and sat down round the Queen, who was seated on a very fine mat, with two very handsome Young Ladies standing by her. In the Middle of the Ring, when the Dinner was laid down before the Queen, all the Servants that brought it stood round, and the Queen ordered the two Young Ladies that stood by her, to serve it out in dishes, then delivered it to the Servants, who Served those who sat round, beginning at them who sat next the Queen. They appeared to be the people of the first Rank. When they were served, every one of them seemed a little grave, and muttered a few words with their faces towards the Sun, then laid or rather threw by a small portion out of Each Dish; after that they began to Eat very hearty. Then the rest of the people was all Served round according to their rank, and the Whole Eat very hearty.

After the Whole of the Grandees was served, there came in three dishes of meat Dressed after another manner, and not like any of the first. This was set down before the Queen, who invited Mr Pickersgill and the Serjeant to Eat with her, but they Excused themselves and pointed to some fresh fruit which was Just pulled off the trees, Choosing that rather nor partake of what seemed to be dressed for the Queen's own Eating. When she found they would not Eat with her, She Ordered the two Young Ladies to feed her, which they did. The one stood at the Right Hand and the other at the left, and fed her by turns with their hands only. She that stood at the Right Hand put her hand in a basin of clean water, then took up a part of the meat, and put it in the Queen's mouth, with her Right hand, and she Eat the meat off her fingers; then the Young Lady washed her hand in Another Basin of Clean

100

water, and stood ready to give her another Mouthful; after she on the Left went through the same Ceremony in this Manner they fed her by turns, but always took great care to wash every time with a basin of Clean Water. He said she Eat very hearty, but touched no meat with her own hands.

After the Queen dined the two young Ladies sat down at a little distance from her, and Eat their own Dinner, Attended by a Great many Young Women. After that all the servants sat down and dined at a great distance from the Ring. Mr Pickersgill supposes the whole Entertainment took little more than an Hour, and he supposes there was between four and five hundred people Dined. He say they all Washed before and After meat, and observed a Strict Silence all the time of dinner, and Seemed to Conduct the whole with great Ease, and every one appeared cheerful and merry.

[Ben Butler's Journal this day records the severest punishment inflicted at Tahiti. James Proctor, Corporal of Marines, had twelve lashes for drunkenness and quarrelling. Furneaux says he struck the Master at Arms in the execution of his office, and Captain Wallis says he also 'left his station'. He was given another twelve lashes the following day.]

*20 July* AFTER all was dined the Queen stood up and made a talk to her people, then ordered two of her people to conduct our people to the landing-place, which they did, and was paid with nails for their trouble.

Soon after the Queen came On board with Six of her chief men, which we Entertained in the Gun-Room. The Captain being very poorly at the time she came On board, we could not carry her Majesty to the Great Cabin. She brought a very good present of live-stock On board, which Served all hands two days, and the Captain ordered her a present in return. The principal part of her Attendants Eat and Drank very hearty with us in the Gun-room but the Queen did neither. She was well Entertained with viewing our Curiosities, while her Great men was busy in Eating and drinking. Each of them Eat hearty and drunk two Glasses of Madeira and a tumbler of Water, but would not Drink either Rum or Brandy Grog. After they took refreshment we Showed them Every part of the Ship upon deck, and in the Galley, which pleased them all very much.

At the time we carried them into the Galley, there happened to be a Pig and two fowl roosting. This they all viewed very Attentively and Laughed very hearty. One of the Men laid hold of the Spit and turned it round three times, then Examined the Cook's Coppers which was Extremely clean, and shone as bright as any tea-kettle in London. This Seemed to Surprise them the most of anything which we showed them. They tried to haul off a small piece of the Copper but could not, then they had a long talk, and the Queen put her hand into both coppers, and seemed Greatly Surprised. We Endeavoured to Explain the use of the Coppers which they seemed to Understand, then Walked aft to the Quarter-Deck where we showed them Geese and Turkeys in the coops. They looked at them and had a good deal of talk, but seemed very little Surprised at the sight of them, which made us suppose they had seen such fowls before, but we never saw any of the kind in the Country, for which reason we gave them a brood of Each some days before we sailed from the Island. We then pointed to the rigging which Surprised them the most of anything.

In my opinion the whole was Smart Sensible people and very curious in observing everything which they saw, but the Queen was rather more so nor any of the rest. She Endeavoured to know the use of most things which we showed her. She is a strong well-made Woman about five foot ten Inches high, and very plainly dressed without either Shoes, Stockings or head dress, and no kind of Jewels or trinkets about her, but the Serjeant says She had three very large Pearls in Each Ear, when he first saw her, but she soon after took them out of her Ears. Her Clothes was Different from the Rest, but worn after the same manner. Her under-garments was white, which

I shall call her Skirt. Her petticoat was White and Yellow, and her Gown was Red, which was the Mourning, which she wore for her Husband, who was killed in the Great double Canoe which gave the Signal for the Attack when they thought to have taken our Ship from us.[1] She appeared very cheerful and merry all the time she was On board.

A little before Sunset the Captain Ordered his Barge to be manned to take an Airing Ashore, and carried the Queen and two of her head men along with him; the other chiefs or head men went in their own Canoes; they were all dressed in White, and no sort of Jewel or trinkets about them, but I observed all their Ears bored, which makes me suppose they wear some sort of trinkets at other times; suppose they had none now. When the Barge Landed there was several hundreds of the Natives Assembled to receive their Queen. When she Landed they all formed a Ring Round her and she made a Long Speech to them, and all the people gave great Attention, not a Whisper was heard while she spoke. When she ended her Speech she pointed to the Captain and all the Officers who was along with him, and made her people understand that they were the principal people belonging to the Ship. She then took her Leave with a short speech, and marched off with a great number of the people Attending her.

Both the Queen and all her Attendants Went off Extremely well pleased with the reception they got on board the ship. As a Confirmation of this, we got more Stock this afternoon nor any three days before. In all we got forty-Eight Hogs and pigs, four dozen of fowls, and a great Quantity of all sorts of fruit.

At night we had fine pleasant weather with some refreshing Showers. Saw great numbers of Lights on both Reefs, and Several fishing along shore. At Sunrise we sent our traders and Liberty men ashore, who had very great success in the trading way. The Current prices this day was a Nine or Seven inch Spike nail for a Hog of fifty or Sixty pounds weight, two forty-penny nails for one of thirty or forty pounds weight, two thirty-

[1] Her red dress was ceremonial and she was not, in fact, in mourning.

penny Nails for one of ten or twenty pounds weight, a thirty or forty-penny nail for a good Roasting pig, a twenty-penny Nail for a good fat fowl, and sixpenny nails and toys bought fruit, and curiosities, such as Shells, hooks etc.

The Gunner told me this day that the old trade is rose about a hundred per cent. This made me Enquire how the people came by the nails. I therefore sent for the carpenter and desired him to Examine his stock of nails. He told me he had and took Care to keep the people from thieving them. We this Day got off twenty-seven Hogs and pigs, Six fowls and some fruit.

*21 July* WE had Moderate fine pleasant weather, with regular Sea and Land breezes. After dinner we sent the traders and Waterers Ashore, but when I was Ordering the liberty men into the boat the Carpenter came and told me every cleat in the Ship was drawn, and all the Nails carried off. At same time the Boatswain informed me that most of the hammock-nails was drawn, and two-thirds of the men obliged to lie on the Deck for want of nails to hang their Hammocks. I immediately stopped the liberty men, and Called all hands, and let them know that no man in the Ship should have Liberty to go Ashore until they informed me who drew the nails and cleats, and let me know what use they made of them: but not one would Acknowledge, that they knew anything about drawing the Nails and Cleats, but all said they knew what use they went to.

I told them it was very Surprising that they knew the use they were put to, but knew none of the men.

Then some of the Young Gentlemen told me, that all the Liberty men carried on a trade with the Young Girls, who had now raised their price for some Days past, from a twenty or thirty-penny nail, to a forty-penny, and some was so Extravagant as to demand a Seven or nine Inch Spike. This was a plain proof of the way the large nails went.

I then Acquainted the Captain of what had happened, and

he ordered me to stop their Liberty, until I found out some of those who had drawn the cleats, then to acquaint him and he would order them all to be punished. I then went upon deck and told all the Ship's Company that there was no man to have liberty, to set his foot upon shore, until I was informed who drew the Nails and cleats.

I then ordered off the boats, who had pretty good success in the trading way. At Sunset they returned On Board and brought off Eight Hogs and Pigs, Six fowls and great plenty of fruit. At Night we had fine pleasant weather, with some refreshing showers.

This evening I observed a great murmuring amongst the people, I therefore stepped forward to see if I could find out who had drawn the nails and cleats. At this time the Galley was full, dressing their Suppers, and some blamed one some Another. It being dark none of them observed me, therefore told their mind plain. At last I found out that the most of them was concerned, and several said they had rather receive a dozen Lashes nor have their liberty Stopped. At last there was a trial amongst them, and six was condemned for spoiling the old trade by giving large Spike nails, when others had only a Hammock-nail, which three declared was refused, they being much smaller nor the Spikes. But two cleared themselves by proving that they got double value for the Spikes. After that a battle ensued, about the one interfering with the other in the way of trade, that obliged me to call out what was the matter, and all was quiet immediately.

At Sunrise I sent all the Boats ashore, but sent no liberty men.

At Noon the boats returned and brought off ten Hogs, Six fowls and plenty of fruit. I told the traders they were to go Ashore after dinner, but none should go on Liberty unless some of them who drew the nails was found out.

At last three concurring Witnesses proved that a poor fellow [Pinkney], who was flogged some time before for thieving, had drawn one of the cleats. This unhappy fellow was a proper object to make an Example of. I therefore Acquainted the

Captain, who ordered me to cause him run the Gauntlet, three times round the Ship. I then called all hands and placed the men in proper order with a nettle in Each of their hands. I several times asked him if there was any of the rest Concerned with him, but he still said no. This made the men very merciful the first round, but when I ordered him the Second round he began to impeach some of the rest, and hoped to be excused himself. I told him it was then too late, and sent him the second round, but the poor fellow got a hard drubbing that time, which made me excuse him from going the third time. At the same time I acquainted the whole that if any such Complaint came again they might rely on a much severer punishment, and none of them would be ever allowed to go on Liberty any more. Then they all declared to a man that they should take great care that no such thing should ever be done again.

*22 July* WE had Moderate clear Weather with the Wind at East. After dinner we sent the traders Ashore and gave Liberty to twenty men as usual. At Sunset the boats returned with Eight Hogs and some fruit. There was no complaints lodged this evening. At Night we had fine clear weather with some refreshing Showers. Saw great numbers of Lights on both reefs and several along shore.

At sunrise we sent the traders and Liberty men Ashore. At Eight A.M. the Queen paid us Another Visit and brought off a very good Present of Live Stock, for which the Captain gave her Another present in return. I convoyed her and one of her principal Attendants into the great Cabin, where the Captain ordered breakfast to be got immediately, and made her and the chief both sit down to tea and Bread and butter: but before the chief touched the bread and Butter he rose up and made a long speech, looking all round the Cabin, then went to the Quarter-Galley and Looked out towards the Sun and kept still talking, which makes me suppose they Worship the Sun. When his talk or Speech was over he sat down on the

Queen's left hand and took up a piece of Soft bread and smelt it, then began to Eat hearty.

We gave him a knife and showed him how to spread the butter on the bread, but He mistook our meaning and laid down the knife, and took up a little of the butter, with the nails of his two foremost fingers and smelt it, then threw it down I suppose according to the custom of his country, as they were always observed to throw away a little of everything they Eat. This put one that was present out of humour, and he was so rude that he snatched the Butter away, and ordered the Captain's Servant to bring clean Butter. This behaviour surprised the chief and prevented him from Eating any more; it likewise made the Queen very Grave, who was very merry before. This made the Captain very uneasy, but he said nothing to old Growl, and soon after made the Queen a present which made her good humoured, but she neither eat nor drank while she was On board.

After Breakfast I carried her all round betwixt decks, where she took very particular notice of everything she saw, and seemed highly pleased. I then carried her into every cabin of the Gun-room, where I showed her everything that was curious, and made her a present of any trinket that she seemed fond of, such as a Looking-Glass, a wine-Glass, buttons and Earrings etc.—but what she seemed most fond of was Linen Cloth. I therefore gave her a very Good Ruffled Shirt, and showed her how to put it on. This trifling present gained her heart, and I convoyed her to the Captain's Cabin, where I left her in great Spirits and the Captain Showed her all his curiosities, but the Queen looking upon him as our King wanted him to Sign a Treaty of Peace in order to settle all Differences betwixt her Majesty's people and ours. But the Captain at that time being very poorly and having a little paralytic disorder in his hand could not hold the pen, therefore Excused himself until another opportunity.

They have a very particular Custom in this country, which is this: at the age of Sixteen they paint all the men's thighs Black, and soon after paint curious figures on their Legs and Arms, and the Ladies seem not to exceed the age of twelve or thirteen when they go through that operation. I suppose they look upon themselves as men and Women at the age of sixteen and twelve.[1]

When I again went into the Captain's cabin the Queen took it into her head that I was painted after the manner of her country, therefore wanted to see my legs, thighs and Arms, and rather nor disoblige her I showed her all, which greatly surprised her and she would not believe that I showed my skin until she felt it with her own hands. She then wanted to see my breast which I likewise showed her, but it surprised her most of all my breast being full of hair. She supposed I was a very strong man and Certainly of Age altho' not painted. She then began to feel my thighs and legs to know if they had the Strength that they seemed to have. I then put my legs in position that they felt both stiff and strong, which made her look very hard in my face, and called out with Admiration, Oh, Oh, Oh, and desired the Chief to feel my legs, which I allowed him to do, and he seemed greatly Astonished as well as She.

After that they had a long talk, and the Queen laid hold of me to lift me up, but I prevented her, without her being Sensible of the reason why she could not lift me up. This Surprised her most of all, and she called Oh Oh and talked again for some time to the chief, who made a Sign for me to Lift her, which I did with one Arm, and carried her round the Cabin. This seemed to please her greatly and She Eyed me all round and began to be very merry and cheerful, and, if I am not mistaken by her Majesty's behaviour afterwards, this is the way the Ladies here try the men, before they Admit them to be their Lovers.

After all this Exercise I suppose she began to be hungry, as She would neither Eat nor drink On board the Ship. She

[1] Tattooing was executed by rubbing soot into punctures made by a serrated instrument. Although accompanied by social ceremonies, it was not an initiation rite. A boy was regarded as a man from weaning, i.e. as soon as he could eat men's food, and was prevented by the food *tapu* from eating with women. Girls married at the age of 12 or 13; boys at 15 or 16.

therefore made Signs that she wanted to go Ashore, and I acquainted the Captain who desired me to take the Barge and carry her Ashore, and to see her home to her Palace, but not to stay any time, as he and both the Lieuts. was in a bad state of health. This was something very Surprising, that all our principal Officers was in so bad a state of health. And at the same time all the Poor Seamen was thoroughly recovered Except one poor man who seemed to be in a decaying state ever since we left the Straits of Magellan.

When I landed her Majesty there was some hundreds of her Subjects standing ready on the Water-side to receive her. After we was carried over the River she laid hold of my hand, and introduced me to all the principal people, and made them all shake hands with me, and one of the Young Gentlemen that I took along with me. After that ceremony was over I ordered Six of the Barge men Armed to come up After us. We then set out Arm-in-Arm for the Palace, and all the Principal part of the Inhabitants came after us. When we got in Sight of the Palace a great number of people came out to receive us, and the Young Gentleman and I shook hands with all those which the Queen pointed out. Then the Queen made a long speech, and all the people formed a Ring round us and Seemed highly pleased.

After the Speech there was a very fine meal spread, and she took the Young Gentleman and I by the hand, and we all three sat down on the Mat. She then made Another Speech and a great number of the principal people Stood round, and gave great Attention to what she said. After that they all talked to one another and seemed Extremely well pleased. Just as we was rising, an old Grave-looking Woman came in very well dressed. On Seeing her the Queen made us sit down again and this old Lady sit down facing us on Another Mat. The Queen and her talked some time together, then the Old Woman moved close by me and felt my Legs and thighs After the same manner that the Queen did, and looked at my hairy breast. This made the old Lady call out with surprise Oh. Oh. Then she and I shook hands, and the old Woman turned very merry and made Signs for me and the Young Gentleman to stay and Dine, but my duty requiring me to go On board, I rose up and made Signs that I could not stay to Dinner—but they did not seem to Understand me at first.

I then Walked round the palace to view it, and measured the length of it with my Broad-Sword, and found it to be a House of three hundred and twenty-one foot Long, and thirty-six foot Broad, neatly built and supported with fourteen large pillars of Wood, in the middle of the House. Every pillar was about fifteen or sixteen Inches diameter and about twenty-four foot high. Several of them was very neatly carved, considering the tools which we saw them have.

While I was viewing the Palace a fine brisk young man came up to me, which the Queen seemed to take notice of. He held out his hand and I shook hands with him. He then wanted to look at my broad-Sword, which I was rather unwilling to give him, but on the Queen's making a Sign to let him have it, I gave it out of my hands, but took care to keep one of my pistols cocked ready in my hand. The Young fellow viewed it all over and felt the Edge, then began to cut capers not unlike one of the Moorfields Cudgel players.[1] This made me a little uneasy and I held out my hand to get the Sword Back, but the stout Young fellow Laughed at me and cut another caper. I then caught hold of his wrist, and took the Sword out of his hand, but not without some trouble. This made him look a little surly, I therefore gave him a Stroke with the flat of the Sword, and immediately turned round and made a Stroke at a plantain tree which was growing close by where we stood, and had the Good luck to cut it through, which so frightened the fellow that he marched off directly. Then the Queen and the old Lady Laughed very hearty, and all the rest smiled and seemed pleased.

I then walked into the Palace, and saw three people beating up some sort of Grease thing, that looked like new made

[1] *Cudgel-playing:* fencing with thick sticks or cudgels. Moorfields, in Finsbury, was once a rendezvous for such sport.

Butter,[1] and several others pulling fruit for dinner. I likewise saw several people carrying small pigs and some fowls to a place at a little distance where there was a great smoke. I suppose they were intended for Dinner, but had not time to go and see how they dressed it. I went to take my Leave of the Queen and the old Lady, but they obliged me to sit down again and the Queen cut me out a Suit of the country cloth, and wanted me to throw off my own, but I declined that and put them on over my own. She wanted me to put on a Second piece, but I refused that, and pointed to the Young Gentleman, and she put that on him. There was no great trouble in making this Suit. She only cut off about ten foot of the piece of Cloth, which was about five foot wide—and cut a hole in the Middle, thro' which hole I put my head; and she then tied it round my waist with a Sash of much finer cloth, then made a Short Speech to her people, who seemed very happy, and gave me a piece of very fine cloth made up snug. It was about sixteen yards long and three Broad.

By that time dinner was near ready, and the Queen insisted on our staying to dinner, but as I had positive orders from the Captain I was obliged to deprive myself of the honour of dining with her Majesty. When she found I was positive to go, She spoke to the old Woman, which I cannot help thinking was her Mother, as She suffered none other to take the least Liberty with her. Then the old Lady laid hold of me, and Endeavoured to detain me, and when she found nothing would prevail on me to stay to dinner, She made me understand with very plain Signs, that I should have her Daughter to Sleep with, and when that had not the desired Effect, the old Lady pointed to two very handsome Young Ladies, and made us understand that the Young Gentleman and I should have them to sleep with, thinking that would tempt us to stay. I then Excused myself in the best Manner I could, and Laid hold of the Queen's hand and the old Lady's to take my leave, at same

[1] This was a paste or pudding, usually made from the root of the edible arum lily (*calodium esculentum*). The flour, produced by pounding, was mixed with water and fermented.

time made them understand that I would soon come Back from my Own Country and Sleep with her in my Arms. This pleased both, and I parted with the old Lady, who seemed extremely well pleased, but the Queen laid hold of my Arm, and Came along with me down to the Water side.

Betwixt the Palace and the Water side there was several Houses full of the principal people of the Island, which I suppose had come down from the Country to see our Ship. She obliged me to call at every House, and I shook hands with all the other people, and was very merry with the Young, as was my Young friend, and the Country people seeing us both dressed after the country fashion, appeared to be very cheerful and happy, and all paid a very great respect to the Queen.

At the last House where we Called, there was two of the handsomest Young Ladies that I ever saw upon the Island. One in particular was fully as fair and had as Good features as the Generality of Women in England. Had she been dressed after the English manner, I am certain no man would have thought her of Another Country. I first shook hands with two fine Jolly old people, which I suppose was the Young Ladies' parents; but they were both of a Mulatto colour. I then shook hands with the Young Ladies, who was both fine brisk spirited women. The fairest, seeing that I took more notice of her than the other, began to be very Merry and we compared skins, and hers was rather fairer and Whiter nor mine. In short I took so much notice of this fine Young Lady that I had almost forgot her Majesty, who was conversing with the old people; but on her looking round and Observing my Young friend deeply engaged with the other young Lady and me seemingly so fond of her which was so very fair, this put the Queen a little out of humour, and she immediately broke up the conversation with the old people and Said something to the young Lady which I was talking with that made her very unhappy. I was sorry to see the Young Lady uneasy, and took her in my Arms to Comfort her—but the instant I laid hold of her, the Queen laid hold of my arm, and gave the poor Young Lady so cross a look in the face, that I really believe she soon after fainted. This really made me a Little unhappy, but know-ing it was my duty to please the Queen, I endeavoured to recover my surprise, and did all I could to please her Majesty, but After that she would enter no House, but in a manner Led me to the boat side, where she waited until I went off to the ship.

This day our traders brought off twelve Hogs, some fowls and plenty of fruit, which not only Served all the Ship's Com-pany but left plenty of fruit to feed the Hogs which we put by to Carry to Sea.

*23 July* WE had a fresh Gale and cloudy weather, with the Wind Easterly. The first part of the day we sent no boats Ashore. At Night we had a Moderate Gale and Cloudy Rainy Weather. We saw no Light on Either reefs nor none along-shore. At Sunrise we Sent the traders, Wooders and Waterers Ashore, and after breakfast sent twenty Liberty men Ashore. At Noon all our boats returned On board and brought off six Hogs and some fruit. There was but few of the Natives came down to trade this forenoon, which I suppose was owing to the rainy morning.

*24 July* WE had fresh Gales with some Squally Showers of Rain, the Wind at ESE. After dinner we sent the trading party Ashore, who brought off six pigs and some fruit. A little before sunset the Captain and first Lieut., with the Surgeon to Attend them, went Ashore to take the Country Air—but Mr Furneaux the Second Lieut. was Extremely bad.

This day I chanced to Look to an Ephemerides [1] which informed me that there was an Eclipse of the Sun on the 25th Inst. which was said to be visible in Mexico and Peru, but not in any part of Europe. By the same Ephemerides it was said to be New Moon at Paris at Seven hours Eight minutes in the Afternoon, for which reason I found it must be Visible where we was. About Seven or Eight next morning, therefore, I Acquainted the Captain who Ordered me to fix the Reflecting telescope and see if it was fit to observe by. This I did but found there was no Dark Glass, belonging to the telescope, for which reason I found it was impossible to observe an Eclipse of the Sun; but on recollecting we found a dark Glass in a small telescope, belonging to a Sextant which the Captain had. This I fitted to the largest telescope, and told the Captain that the Instrument was ready. He then ordered me to take the Barge and go to observe the Eclipse at the proper time.[2]

At Night we had a fresh Gale and Cloudy weather with some Rain, but the morning was clear weather. We sent the traders and liberty men Ashore, who carried on trade as usual, and brought off six Hogs, and some fruit, and a great Quantity of Shells, Mother-of-Pearl fish-hooks and a few pearls.

[As the time for departure was approaching, Captain Wallis decided this day to send the Queen an important and representative series of presents. They included: 'two Turkeys, two geese, three guinea-hens, a cat big with kitten, some china, looking-glasses, glass bottles, shirts, needles, thread, cloth, ribands, peas, some small white kidney beans called callivances, different sorts of garden seeds, and a shovel, besides a considerable quantity of cutlery ware, consisting of knives, scissors, bill-hooks and other things including 2 iron pots and a few spoons'.]

[1] An astronomical almanac.

[2] Observations of eclipses had to be made on shore, the ship's motion making it impracticable to keep the object continuously in the field of view of the telescope.

*25 July* WE had Moderate fine pleasant weather with the Wind Easterly. After dinner we sent the Boats a-trading and got off Eight Hogs, some fowls and plenty of fruit. A little before Sunset the Captain and 1st Lieut. went Ashore for the benefit of the country air. My old friend meet with his little handsome woman, who brought him down a fine fat pig, which he paid her for, but took no notice of the Signal which formerly he was so ready to obey; he said he could not help thinking of the Risk the poor Carpenter run, when she made him jump overboard at the Mercy of the ravenous Sharks. He says the Guard went on in the old way, regularly relieving one another and getting value for their nails.

At Sunset the Barge returned with some fowls, two pigs and a few bunches of Plantains and Bananas; At Night we had fine pleasant weather. Saw great numbers of people on both reefs fishing.

At Sunrise I got all ready to go and observe the Eclipse with Mr Harrison the Purser and Mr Pinnock, one of the Young Gentlemen along with me. But the instant we was going into the Boat, Old Growl got up a great deal sooner nor his Ordinary and stopped us, telling me he was Surprised how I could take the barge without acquainting him. I let him know it was the Captain's orders, and if he stopped me now, I must acquaint the Captain as the Eclipse would be over before I got Ashore.

He told me he knew the Captain's Orders, and gave me a disdainful sneer, and Ordered Mr Gore with a party of twenty Armed men into the Barge, Cutter and Launch, then told me I might take the Jolly-boat, if I wanted to look at the Sun, with an instrument that I knowed nothing about. I thanked him for his civility and ordered up the Jolly-boat's crew to shift the things out of the Barge into the Jolly-boat, but old Growl found ways and means to detain us too long—but knowing him to be a Ill-natured Ignorant sort of Man, I said nothing more to him but got Ashore as fast as possible to the Northern-most point of the Bay, Where I desired Mr Pinnock to take the Altitude of the Sun, and work the true time of the Day.

At same time Mr Harrison and I took the instant of time that he observed the Sun's altitude, by our Watches, which was regulated the night before. When that was done Mr Harrison began to look at the Sun with a very good Spy-Glass, and told me he thought the Eclipse was beginning. Mean-time I was fixing the Reflecting telescope, and bid him observe the time by his Watch, which he did and found it to be about $6^h : 51' : 50''$. At same time Mr Pinnock took the Sun's altitude, which Corresponded with the Watch.

In about two minutes after Mr Harrison first Observed the Eclipse, I got the Reflecting telescope fixed, and saw that the Immersion [1] had commenced some minutes sooner nor Mr Harrison observed it. This was owing to our being so long detained by Old Growl. I must own I was very unhappy as was both my companions for fear of our not being able to determine the Immersion, as the weather was beginning to be very cloudy. But we chanced to have better fortune, for the weather proved very clear all the time of the Eclipse. When the Eclipse was near ended I desired Mr Pinnock to run and acquaint the Captain that it was near over, he being at that time coming along shore in his Barge, with old Growl along with him, who I dare say prevailed on him to come ashore to Laugh at my Ignorance, in pretending to know what time the Eclipse happened.

When Mr Pinnock acquainted the Captain, old Growl gave a disdainful Sneer, and said he supposed the Captain would come time Enough to see it ended as it was not yet began, because he could not discover it with his Sickly Eyes; but the Young Gentleman told the Captain that he saw it for some time himself, and that I desired him to acquaint the Captain that if he wanted to look at it, he must make haste. Then they all came up, and saw it both with the telescope, and the Common Spy-Glass.

This made the Captain very happy, and he desired me to

[1] *Immersion:* the time at which the appearance of the sun was concealed. Robertson, by this and other observations, hoped to determine his longitude, which was always difficult before the making of accurate chronometers.

be very Exact in observing the end of the Eclipse, which I did with the Greatest Exactness, but not without some difficulty with old Growl, who still keep reflecting on me, and declaring that I saw nothing of the Eclipse with the Reflecting telescope, because he could not see with so nice an Instrument. But he owned that he saw it very plain with Mr Harrison's spy-Glass. I begged him to have a little patience until the Eclipse was over.

I then told Mr Pinnock to be ready to take the Sun Altitude. At the same instant that I called to him, at same time desired Mr Harrison to be very Exact in observing the end by his common Glass, which he did, and called out directly, but I having so fine an Instrument could see it continue about a minute longer before the tops of the Mountains disappeared on the Verge of the Sun.

Old Growl at this time did me some service, tho' un-designedly; he insisted on Mr Pinnock's taking the Sun Altitude, the very Instant that Mr Harrison called the Eclipse was over. But he expecting Orders from me was not ready, until the Instant that I called stop. This was a very lucky circumstance, for I forgot to give Mr Pinnock timely notice, being a little perplexed with the ungenteel behaviour of old Growl; so that by the assistance of this ill-natured man, I dare say we ascertained the time of the Immersion within a Second of the true time, both by the Sun and by the Watches. So that the time of the duration of this Eclipse, was nearly one hour nine minutes and ten seconds; but the Immersion is not to be depended on within less nor two or three minutes, but the Immersion may be relied on with Great Exactness which happened at $8^h : 1' : 00''$ Log time, the 25th of July A.M. Or to reckon by Astronomical time, the Immersion Commenced the twenty-fourth at Eighteen hours fifty-one minutes and fifty seconds nearly, and Ended Exactly at twenty hours one minute.[1]

For fear of some of my Readers Judging as illnaturedly as old

[1] Robertson omits the results of his observations, which were 17° 30′ S., 150° W. Captain Cook calculated the position as 17° 29′ 15″ S., 149° 32′ 30″ W. and commends the accuracy of the observations taken in the *Dolphin*.

Growl, and suppose, as he did, that I could not see the Sun any Longer Eclipsed nor Mr Harrison did with the Common Spy-Glass, Let them be pleased to observe that the telescope which I observed with, Magnified the object about two hundred times more nor any man's Eye, and most people know how much a Common Spy-Glass Magnifies more than the Eye. It's likewise known to all those who ever used to view the Moon with so good a telescope as this was, that the Surface of the Moon Appears uneven, and the top of the Mountains can be plainly discovered on the Verge of the Sun. With a common Spy-Glass the Moon appears quite round, but with this telescope the verge of the Moon looked like the top of a Wood betwixt us and the Sky, that is supposing the highest trees to be mountains. I observed two keep betwixt me and the Sun when Mr Harrison called it was over, therefore I did not call stop, until the instant that the two mountains disappeared. The Easternmost of the two appeared to be the Largest, and Looked not unlike the top of a small tree, betwixt you and the sky when growing on a high Mountain.

Just as we had done with the Observation, the Queen and one of her chiefs came to us, and I gave her a sight of the Sun with the dark Glass, which Surprised beyond Expectation both her and her Chief, who likeways had a sight.

As near as I could suppose the Sun was Eclipsed about two Digits, that interrupted the Light of the Sun so little, that no man could observe it with his naked Eye, therefore the Natives of this Island knew nothing of the Matter. Had this been a total Eclipse I dare say we might have got what we pleased from the poor Natives, as did the Great Columbus in the Island of Jamaica on the like occasion.

I then turned the telescope to the SW point of the Bay and made the Queen and her chief look through at their friends about five miles off. This Surprised them beyond measure, and the chief wanted to have another look at the Sun. I set the telescope, but neglected putting in the dark Glass, which almost blinded the poor man. But to keep him from knowing the trick, I put in the dark Glass and looked as long as he, then

118

Looked him full in the face as if I had been Surprised at his not being able to look.

After this I went on board and put by the Instruments, In hopes of being able to determine the Longitude of Some other places, with this fine telescope, by observing the Satellites of Jupiter: but in that I was greatly disappointed, as we touched at no other place in the South Sea but the Island of Tinian, and at that time the Planet Jupiter was so near the Sun, that I could not observe the Satellites—and at the other Places where we touched going home, I was prevented by other Reasons.

This Day Mr Gore with twenty Armed men went to discover the inland Country. At Seven A.M. the party set out from the River Mouth, and Marched up the River-side about five or six mile, where they found great numbers of Inhabitants, and great plenty of fruit trees such as Bread-fruits, Apples, Plantains and Bananas, Likewise several other trees with fruits that none of our Men was acquainted with. Mr Gore and his party Dined Near the River mouth, and the traders at the Market place; they sent us off fourteen Hogs, Some fowls and plenty of fruit.

*26 July*  WE had Moderate fine pleasant weather with a regular Sea and Land Breeze. After dinner Mr Gore's party set out again on discoveries, and at sunset returned On board And brought off Several different kinds of fruit, that none of the party knew any name for; they likewise brought off several sorts of Roots which we knew no name for, except Ginger. Mr. Gore told me that he saw great plenty of Cotton and Indigo growing up the Country. I suppose the finest sort of their cloth is made of Cotton and the coarser is made out of the Bark of a small Willow, which they raise up very carefully in Nurseries. He Likewise brought off some pieces of Rock which he said he Supposed Contained some sort of Metal.

The pieces of Rock were Black and very Weighty. The whole was delivered to the Captain and I hope when tried at old England they will turn out to be of great Value. This was the first and Last Attempt that we ever made to discover the Inland Country—and Mr Gore and all the people acknowledged that the Natives behaved with the Greatest discretion. They stood pilot, and showed them the best road, when they went into a wrong path; they put them soon in the right way, and not only gave them Victuals to Eat, but carried Water in cocoa-Nuts and Bamboos for them to drink and Served them to carry their Luggage of all Sorts.

This evening we saw a great many large vessels come round the SW point of the Bay and go into the same Place where we observed the Great fleet go into, with all their Streamers flying, But where these Great Vessels came from, or what Cargoes they Contained is more nor I can tell, as I never had it in my power to visit the Place where they went into. At Night we had fine pleasant weather with some refreshing Showers. Saw great numbers of people on both reefs fishing, and Several along shore.

At Sunrise sent all our traders Ashore. Soon after the Captain and 1st Lieut. went Ashore for the benefit of their health, with the Surgeon along with them, but the Second Lieut. was confined to his bed in a very bad State of health. This Morning we began to clear the Ship for the Sea, and bent several of our sails which had been unbent to repair.

There came a Large double canoe from the SW point of the Bay, with three of the fairest Strong well-made men that I have yet seen on all the Island. They were paddled off by Eight of the Red sort of people. When they came along-Side they were very Merry and Cheerful, and Seemed to want to be aboard of the ship. I then made Signs for them to come in, which they did Immediately, but took care to hand in three fine Hogs of forty or fifty pounds weight before they came out of the Canoe.

Then they came up very cheerful and Shook hands with me on the Quarter-Deck. They appeared to be three brothers; the oldest seemed to be about thirty and the youngest about two or four and twenty years of age. Just as they came in we was ready to haul up the Main-sail to bend it to the yard. I made Signs to them to Assist us, which they did, and pulled hearty until

120

the Sail was up to the Yard, then the two youngest went up the Shrouds and went upon the yard and assisted in bending the Sail, but the oldest Brother Stayed with me, and I paid him for his three Hogs. This appeared to be a very Sensible Curious sort of Man. He took very particular notice of everything he saw.

I enquired of all our people if any of them had ever seen any of these three Brothers Ashore, but they all said they never saw any of them.

I then tried if this man could Let me know where he Lived. He seemed to understand me, and Pointed to the SW end of the Bay, then waved his hand farther, and Laughed, then made Signs for me to come and Sleep at the place where he lived. I then Endeavoured to make him understand that we was soon to come that way with the Ship, then I would come and Sleep at his House. That seemed to please him much, and he called to his two brothers who were coming down the Shrouds. He made them both come up and Shake hands with me, then Endeavoured to make them understand that our Ship was to come to their part of the Country. This pleased the younger Brothers greatly, and they pointed to the point and waved their hands twice, I suppose meaning to make me understand that they lived a great way beyond the SW point of the Bay.

At ten A.M. the Barge returned with the Captain, and the three Brothers went away in their Canoe towards the SW point of the Bay. At Noon our traders returned on board with twenty Hogs and pigs, and a large Quantity of fruit: they likeways purchased several curious things from the Natives, such as Pearls, Pearl Oyster Shells, hooks, Lines for fishing, stone adzes, stone hammers and several other curious things. We purchased several Bows-and-Arrows from the Natives, but scarce saw any that was fit for War, neither did any one of us see them use their Bows-and-Arrows to kill or hurt any creature.[1]

This day the Captain made Signs that we was to Sail to-Morrow, in order to get the Natives to bring down plenty of

[1] More than one of the *Dolphin* Journals expresses surprise that the bow was not used as a serious weapon, but chiefly for killing small animals and birds.

Stock, and Ordered the Gunner, who always stood Market man, to let all the people at the Market-place know that we was to sail the Morrow at Sunrise, and then Endeavour to make them bring down as much as possible of their Hogs, Fowls, fruit etc.

[Captain Wallis, who had by now interested himself in the details of what Robertson calls 'The Old Trade', noted at this point, not without a certain tart reproof: 'Even the fathers and brothers showed Sticks proportionate to the Nail they were to give'—in satisfaction for the favours of the ladies of their family.]

*27 July* WE had fine Moderate pleasant weather with the Wind Easterly. The first part of the day we completed our Water to Seventy-Eight Tuns; and got everything clear for sea. After dinner we sent the Trading party Ashore, who brought off ten large Hogs, several fowls and a Great Quantity of fruit. At 4 P.M. the Queen came On board to Endeavour to make us stay for some Days longer nor we intended; at her first coming on board She appeared very Merry and brought off a very Good present of live-Stock, but the instant that the Captain made her understand that we was to Sail at Sunrise, She appeared greatly Concerned And made Signs for us to stay ten days before we took our departure from her fruitful pleasant Island; but the Captain was positive to Sail next morning, therefore ordered the Ship to be unmoored, that we might be ready to sail the Sooner in the Morning.

When this Great Woman could not prevail with the Captain to stay ten days, she came down to nine, Eight, Seven, Six and five days, and when she found that he still was for going in the Morning at Sunrise, She immediately Wept and Cried for some minutes, then made all the friendly Signs that she could possibly think of to induce us to stay only two days longer. But the Captain would not be prevailed on by her Entreaties, but still made Signs that he would sail at Sunrise.

This positive resolution of the Captain's affected this Great Woman beyond Expectation. When she found that all her entreaties had no Effect She immediately burst out in Tears, and Cried and Wept in such a manner that few men could have helped pitying her. But what reason she had for wanting us to stay a few days longer I know not, but several of my Ship-mates said she had some treacherous design in wanting us to stay a few days longer, therefore thought it best to sail at sunrise next morning for fear of their making fresh Attempts on our Ship or Men, but what reason my Ship-mates had for such uncharitable Conjectures I know not. But this I am certain of, this Great Woman has been our good friend ever since the first day that she came on board our Ship, as a proof of this, Since that time we have got near three times the quantity of all sorts of refreshments, that we did before we became acquainted with her; and the whole of the Natives has placed a much greater confidence in us nor they did before.

They do not seem to have the least suspicion of our defrauding them, neither do I think that they have the least intention of defrauding us, for they have dealt very fair and honestly ever since we became acquainted with the Queen, and the more our people go amongst them they think themselves the happier.

For several days past our Seamen went into the Woods singly and traded with the natives for all sorts of curious things, and no man has ever made the least complaint of the natives Attempting to defraud them, neither did they ever offer to hurt or molest any man, even when they found our men with their Young Girls, some hundred Yards from our Guard. Besides, their behaviour to Mr Gore and his party when they went to discover the Country, all this I think is a very clear proof that they have no treacherous design against us.

In place of having a treacherous design, the Great Woman shook hands with us, and when she found all her tears and entreaties could not prevail with us to stay two days longer she made signs that she would stay and Sleep On board all night, that she might have the pleasure of our Company while we was to stay. But this friendly plan of hers was disapproved of, and she was made to understand that she must go ashore. But to please her we endeavoured to make her understand that we would soon return again to her beautiful Island. This Seemed to please her a little, and we all gave her a few presents, and let her know that the Boat was ready to go Ashore. But the instant she went into the boat, she again fell a-Crying and shedding tears the same as before. In my opinion this Grief of hers proceeded from nothing but her unwillingness to lose our friendship and good Company. When the Barge landed her she made a long speech to her people, and the Officer who was in the barge, told me that all the people seemed greatly concerned, when she told them that we was going away in the morning.

This evening we saw a great many large Canoes come round the SW point of the Bay. We likewise saw great numbers of Lights on the Reef until it was past ten P.M. At 5 A.M. we hove short and sent the Launch for some water. It being calm we could not weigh the Anchor until a fresh Breeze Sprung up. When the Launch and Cutter got close to the Watering place, our people Observed several hundred people on the Beach, which made them unwilling to land, as they never saw them come down before, until the Sun was up.

This made our people suppose, they were now ready to be revenged for the Loss of their Countrymen, which was killed, when the poor unthinking people thought to have made a Prize of the only ship that ever Surrounded the Globe twice. Therefore our men lay on their oars for some time Until they should See how the Natives behaved. But in a few minutes the Queen came down, and made Signs for our men to Land, but they would not until she ordered her people to the other side of the River. Then they landed and filled what casks they had, and soon got them into the Boats and ready to come off.

While this was doing the Queen made the Officers understand that she had Lain on the Beach all Night, with all the people which he saw there along with her. This was with no other intention but to see us again before we Sailed from her fruitful country. When the Officer Stepped into the Boat, the Queen with a few of her principal Attendants wanted to come

124

off with him, but he had orders from the Captain to take none of the Natives on board, therefore came off without her. This he told me made her very unhappy, and She immediately ordered a few of her people to bring her a large double canoe, which was lying at some distance on the Shore.

When our boats came along-side we hoisted in the Water, and got in some Hogs, fowls and fruit, which the Queen made our people a present of, without accepting any present in return. We then Weighed and made Sail, but there was so little wind that we was obliged to tow the ship with the Boats. The Instant that we got under sail the Queen came under the Stern with a large double canoe, and brought us off a great Quantity of More Live Stock and the Captain made her some presents in return. But this Great friendly Woman took no manner of notice of what She got from us, but Shook hands with all that she could come near. She wept and cried, in my opinion with as much tenderness and Affection as any Wife or Mother could do, at the parting with their Husbands or children.

There was Several Large double Canoes came off with her this Morning which came from the SW end of the Bay last night. In Each of these canoes, there was a very Convenient place where ten or a dozen people could sit under a canopy. It was built not unlike the place where the Gentlemen Sits in the City Barges, altho' not so finely decorated. In these Large Canoes there were a great Many families of Jolly fat well-made people, and much fairer nor any that we ever saw before, the two Young Ladies which the Queen introduced me to only Excepted. They were likewise dressed much neater nor any of the people which we saw before. All the Servants which paddled these great Canoes were of a copper colour and their masters and mistresses seemed to have a great power over them. The whole of the fair people sat under the Canopies.

And I observed both the Men and Women have all their Ears bored, but none of them had any sort of Jewellery in their Ears, but I think their Ears being bored, is a clear demonstration that they do wear some sort of Jewellery when at home. I enquired of all our trading party if any of them had ever Seen any of these people before, but they all said they never saw any of them before—neither did any On board ever see so many fair people at one time.

I am of Opinion that these people came from some distant shore, and as we saw several large Canoes, coming round the SW point last Evening, am apt to think that they came from the High Land to the Southward, of this Country.[1] There was one Venerable old Man in one of these canoes, that all the rest paid a particular respect to. He was clothed better nor the rest and Wore a White turban about his head, and a pretty long grey beard.

All the fair people gave great attention to what he said, and the Servants seemed feared when this venerable old man Spoke, but the people of this Bay Seemed not to understand what he said, but all of them looked hard at him and kept clear of the Canoe which he was in. I saw his Servants once paddle his Canoe close to the Queen when the old Man was busy Viewing us making sail. But the instant that he observed his canoe foul of hers, he spoke to his Servants very Angry-like, and made them Sheer his Canoe clear of hers. This was the only piece of respect that I observed him show to her, which makes me suppose this Man was some Chief. This Race of White people in my opinion has a great resemblance to the Jews, which are Scattered through all the known parts of the Earth.

While these people were along-side, I was obliged to take Charge of the Ship, and Carry her out to Sea, therefore could not have time to observe anything else about them, but a few words which the old Man spoke, that I wrote down on a piece of paper, but knew not the meaning of what he said, but am Certain I have heard some such words before, spoken by some people that I have been amongst. But being in a hurry I left the paper on the drum-head of the Capstan, where it was taken away by somebody on board or else thrown over-board. The Red or copper-Coloured people here are Exactly like the Malays in Batavia or Princes Island.

At ten A.M. we got a fine Light breeze Easterly. We lay-to

[1] It is probable that they came from one of the other districts of the island.

about half an hour, and bought a great many fine fat Hoggs, several Fowls and some fruit, then made Sail and Steered away to the Westward, toward the Duke of York's Island, and Left all the Country people who came out with us, in great Sorrow, Especially the Queen and the Most part of our old Acquaintance belonging to the Bay where we lay.

I really do believe there was a vast many of these Country people who would have willingly come home with us, if we could have taken them, and there was some of our Men, who said they would stay at this place, if they were sure of a Ship to come home within a few years.

[Two days later, on 29 July, when the island of the *Dolphin*'s idyll was becoming a happy memory, Captain Wallis noted in his Journal: 'the ship makes more water than she did before. The rudder loose, and shakes the Stern very much.' They had received rather more damage from grounding at Tahiti than Robertson noted. Nevertheless, the frigate returned to England without any further serious misadventure.]